A Mother's Journey Through The Loss Of Her Son

A decade of writing my story, my heart, my faith and my grief that needed to be shared

2010-2020

Barbara A. Barber

joyfulnoiseforajoyfullife.blogspot.com
noni.barber6@gmail
Available on Amazon

Published by: Leona Bjarke
Edited by: Susi Shapter
Covers: Nathaniel Madlem

; Brings hope that your story isn't over yet

Olympic Mountains, Washington -August 97

Foreword

When Ron and I found out that it was absolutely impossible for me to get pregnant, we immediately started working on adoption. People were full of advice about the best way to find a child. We were willing to do anything and everything to start a family. One afternoon, Ron's mom, Mary, was over at our house and said she would help me stuff envelopes to send letters with our picture to OB/GYNs. A few hours went by, and we were having a great chat. She stopped in the middle of licking an envelope and began to laugh. I thought for sure the glue was getting to her. She took my hands, looked me deep in the eyes and assured me that

God had babies out there for us. It touched my heart but didn't explain why she was laughing. She pointed out that essentially by sending letters we were "making a baby," and she never thought she would have an active role in that process. I told her I always thought it would be much more fun. Mary was right about how our family would grow. We ended up having four selfless birth moms choose us to raise their precious children. God had planned just the right family for us. Ron and I didn't "make a baby" in

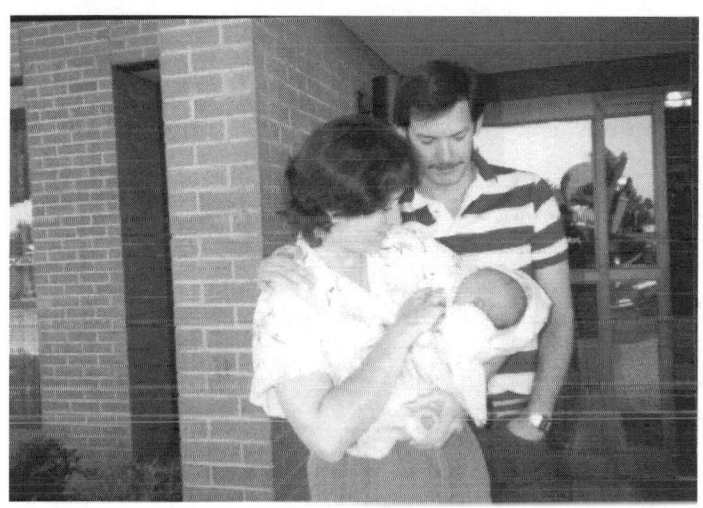

the traditional way, but I would not trade my four wonderful, unique kids for anything. A family is formed through love, one way or another. Ten years ago we lost our second son, Ryan, to suicide. We feel so grateful for the twenty-four years we had him here with us. Each of us has grieved, clung to each other and healed over this past decade. But the hole in our family and in each of our hearts remains where Ryan's bright smile and warm hugs should be. A few months before I lost my son I began this blog. It was God's invaluable gift to me that I had this outlet to write my grief, my faith and my heart. This Christmas a sweet friend took my words and presented me with a book of the posts about losing my

Ryan. It was a clear sign that I was meant to share my journey beyond those who might stumble across my blog. This is a small piece of my blog about the loss of my son. So many more posts have documented our lives as a family and community. Leona, Susi and I have spent the past few months editing and figuring out printing to bring this to you. I would not have had the courage to even read my journey without the encouragement of these two incredible women. So here is a window into my heart through a loss I never imagined I would have to endure as I held my newborns in my arms. This is a testimony of the love and support of my Savior and the people He brought to walk beside me through my life.

In Him,

Joyful

A letter to my son.....ten years later.

Ryan, my son,

How I continue to miss you a decade after you left me! So many times I pause and think you should be here to share this moment with me. Watching Elissa turn sixteen and seeing how loving she is makes me so proud, but also makes my heart ache that you are not here to be a part of her life. So, although I am sure you are on your next adventure in heaven, I wanted to let you know just how I am doing ten years after I had to begin life without you.

I began a blog a few months before you died. Often I called you up to read a post about your antics with your brothers and sister. "Clown Suits and Cowboy Boots" was one of my favorites. You laughed and were glad when I shared our stories with you. That writing carried me through losing you. The day after I lost you, I wrote. I have been writing almost daily ever since. It started out so sad, and my heart was crushed, but it didn't stay that way. As our family grew and healed, I wrote more about life than death. Recently, sweet Leona took the posts about you and gifted me with a book. For years I have had it on my heart to share my faith-walk through losing you. Her gift prompted me to get it completed. Susi and I edited and revised, learning so much along the way. Now, Dad is going to sprinkle in some pictures, Nate and Natalie are designing a cover, and so many have prayed over whose hands my heart words need to end up in. It has been humbling to even contemplate publishing our story. Now I need the courage to finish it.

Ryan, Dad and I have been given a ministry we could have never imagined. Your suicide has moved us to walk beside other parents and families who have lost their own loved ones to suicide or drug overdoses. It is one of the hardest situations we have ever been in. But God steps up with us to be there at the darkest time a family will ever go through, and it matters. I am humbled that we have been chosen for this journey.

Faith and family have surrounded me with love this past decade. Although I miss you more than you could ever know, I am okay. No one calls me beautiful, but so many share heart rocks with me. There are those who are a part of my life because we share a love for you; that is a gift you gave me from above. Ten years ago I couldn't imagine living life without you. What I have come to understand is even though I can't wrap my arms around you, call to make you laugh or simply hear your voice, you are still with me. You died too soon, but you taught each of us to encourage others, laugh at ourselves, and that life is an adventure; also, how to get free pizza in the most awkward ways.

Ryan, I miss you. I wish the last ten years could have been lived with you here with me. I love you, my son. I have never been angry with you for ending your life. You practiced for years, and I don't know that you meant that day in April to be your last. One thing I know for sure is that you didn't pull that trigger out of selfishness or because you didn't love enough. Your heart for others is the truth I live with and the truth I know. There has not been a moment I have worried about you since that day. You are safe and whole, and I am sure heaven is more lively with you there. There is no need for forgiveness, my son, because I never blamed you. Please know that my love for you is even stronger now than it was before. There will be a day where we will enjoy an endless hug in each other's arms, and you will once again call me beautiful. Until then I will enjoy those you gifted me with and keep your Elissa close.

Thank you my son, for sharing your love, your light and your life with me. What a gift to be your mom.

Mom
8-21-20

Ryan wrapped his trip to heaven between my birthday and his sister, Natalie's. He left us on April 5th and gifted us with memories of him, and his overflowing love remains tucked away in our hearts.

TUESDAY, APRIL 6, 2010

Wrapped in the Arms of My God, My Family and Friends

Life will never be quite the same after today. My precious, tormented son took his own life. How can this be? Only faith and our relationships will get us through this heartbreak. Numb, crushed, unable to breathe are a few ways people described their ache. God, you must cradle him in your arms for me now.

Never again will I pick up the phone and hear, "Hello, Beautiful!" I can't stop calling his phone to hear his voice on the other end. This voice that was forever silenced on April 5th. Parents should never have to make arrangements like this. Our kids are supposed to lay us to rest, not the other way around.

God performed a miracle for me the night before I lost my son. I met a cousin of my friend, Jenn, and actually had dinner with her Sunday night after Jenn's surgery. Years ago, her son took his life. I asked her how she possibly survived such a loss. She said it so simply, "By faith."

No big mystery. Just have a continuous, personal relationship with Jesus Christ.

Unbelievably, not even 24 hours later I was faced with the untimely loss of my son. It has been an amazingly long day. "By faith" my family is making it through. Looking at pictures, reliving memories and a whole lot of time spent holding loved ones' hands and kneeling before our Awesome God. This house has not seen prayer of this magnitude in far too long. The good news is, we are putting God at the center of all of this.

Ryan is resting in God's faithful arms tonight, and I am managing a peaceful loneliness while surrounded by my family and friends. There are already countless blessings from Ryan's death as we all come together to celebrate his life. I hope he in some way knows how very much he touched so many.

In Him,
Joyful

WEDNESDAY, APRIL 7, 2010

Our Generous Hometown is my Home

I could not have imagined being where I am today. Yet, here I am, heartbroken and wrapped in the loving arms of my amazing family and friends. The terrible chore of writing my son's obituary was softened with the help of my sister sitting right there by my side. Working out the details of the Life Celebration ended up being a joyful experience with the inclusion of my loving spiritual leaders, my husband and son. Saturday is going to be a treasured day for our little town. Ryan will be the heart and soul of the day as we celebrate his life and his faith in our God.

Am I sad? Exhausted? Numb? Of course! I catch myself carrying on, and then it hits me again that I will never rub his back, never hear him call me "beautiful mother", never hear his laugh, never taste his cleverly created culinary concoctions and never see his eyes smile. Oh God, how hard this truth of my loss is. Thank you for walking me through the tunnel of this pain.

This town has stepped up; actually they have organized an army. Our every need is being taken care of so we are left to share our grief and love with our family who are ascending into our town to just be with us. There is food overflowing into my Cathy's house because no way could it all fit here. My Young Life girls ran over (literally) during their lunch just to give me a hug and tell me they love me. Because of my incredible school family, I was able to feed them a delicious lunch. The lunch after Ryan's goodbye party is all taken care of, and Ron and I don't even have to worry about it. The angels at several churches are teaming up with our school to take care of everything. Cathy has taken on such a leadership role tirelessly fitting everything into place even though she loved Ryan and is grieving too.

Tonight was wonderful with my family here looking through pictures, watching videos, sharing memories and of course eating and drinking the marvelous food. Food that was provided from the love and support of this hometown; our hometown.

My son is gone from my touch, but his life is being celebrated, and this week will be precious to me my whole life. Thank you Ryan, for the love and the knowledge that you are having your own celebration with your loved ones up above.

In Him,
Joyful

FRIDAY, APRIL 9, 2010

Two Parties, One Incredible Son

Swinging my grandson, Timmy, at the park and watching my three beautiful granddaughters, Lissa, Kenzie and Kayla, carry heavy sand buckets to the top of the slide puts the smile back in my heart. There are so many tasks to accomplish for Ryan's special goodbye party on Saturday. At times, we get so busy that I forget why we are so busy. Then Pat reminds me to go to the bathroom, and I have a private moment to myself to think about what all of this is.

Yesterday I was sad for Ryan for not being here to hear all the stories and see all the love. Then I realized he is up in the presence of God, home in

His arms. Up there with him is his crazy Grandpa Harold, and no one was a better party dude than him.

I know he knows that we will all keep Elissa in our hearts and in our arms. And I promise him she will know how much he loved her, and how incredibly special he was. Of course, we will tell her what a little ornery shit he was too. It will be my pleasure to do all I can to help my Lis remember her daddy and his love for her.

Enjoy your party up there Ryan, and give everyone a hug for us. We will celebrate who you are here until we see you again.
In Him,
Joyful Mom

SATURDAY, APRIL 10, 2010

Hard Day, But Not Impossible

Someone came up to me yesterday, gave me a hug and said there is absolutely nothing worse a mother could go through. I began to cry, but then God gave me a peace. This is an enormous tragedy, yet it could be so much worse. I have an assurance that my son is resting in the arms of Jesus. Ryan loved the Lord. Oh, he didn't follow the laid out plan for sure, but he called for prayers and prayed for others. So Ryan knew God walked beside him. The song, "What Faith Can Do" by Kutlass was his "Life Song". One line in particular seemed a challenge to him.
"Impossible is not a word, it's just a reason for someone not to try."

He recognized he needed to try and stop making excuses for his life. When he was giving or helping others in any way there was a different light in his eyes. His crazy concoctions were cooked with love and laughter. There was always enough to share with everyone in the whole neighborhood.

He loved his sweet Elissa. Finally he realized he was not in a healthy enough place to be near her for a while, so he moved away to get sober. Just after Christmas this year they had an incredible week together. Ryan was totally present with his daughter and should get Dad of the Year. She was his whole focus. Ice skating, reading books, sledding with cousins and just sitting holding her while they recalled the good times they had shared made it an unforgettable week for both of them. I thank God for the sweet gift of that week.

This day for me is about all the people Ryan loved and all those who are driving tirelessly to lay on a bit of floor at my house with only one bathroom, just to be here to say goodbye to a man who loved all the people that he met. So for me today there is a verse that will lead me through. My challenge verse that I have tried so long to make it through just one day adhering exactly to is : *Your every action must be done with love.* (1Corinthians 16:14) So far, as I lay my head on my pillow at night, I have fallen short of this ideal. Perhaps today at my sweet Ryan's going away party, will be the day I make it through a whole day with love in my heart for others. *"Impossible is just a reason for me not to try."* Pray for me.

In Him,
Joyfully Heartbroken Mom

SUNDAY, APRIL 11, 2010

Spectacular Goodbye Party

Loved ones filled the church, the program was perfectly put together, tissue for each hand, let the celebration begin to unfold. Lissa began with her special prayer, supported by her mommy, Aunt Nini and Noni. She sang tenderly of courage and comfort from her Lord. Fitting that Ryan's daughter would introduce his life celebration. Then his older brother, Pastor Cameron, took the stage to tell about not only his life but his faith and his new found presence in heaven. Every word spoken was perfect for my ears and all who had gathered. Ron created the most amazing video, played the "He's My Son" song and the church filled with laughter and tears. Scooter was honored and remembered for his love of others, joy of life and his struggles with substances, but also for his love for the Lord. Tom Steward, bless his heart for Ryan, brought home the fact that God does not only receive those who stay on the straight path of life. He explained God's immense mercy and grace for those who struggle and fall. Tanner shared his heart for his brother, his best friend.

Closing this service with Ryan's professed "Life Song": "What Faith Can Do" emphasized that there is hope for us all, and none have strayed too far from God's mercy.

My son is home in heaven wrapped in God's love, urgently getting reacquainted with Connor, his grandfathers, Uncle Dan and holding Aunt Emma's hand so she can meet them all beside him. Ryan didn't miss his life celebration in Los Alamos yesterday. Ryan was chilling in the heavenly celebration of his arrival with those he knew on earth and those he will seek out in heaven.

I know you will make everyone there feel as loved as you made all of us feel loved down here. Gotta say I am going to miss you, but can't say I am sorry for you. Enjoy, my son. I love you.
In Him,
Joyful

MONDAY, APRIL 12, 2010

Dear Ryan

My precious son~Ryan,

Although it is going to be tough going forward living life without you in it, I will do my best. My heart is sure that you did this, not selfishly to hurt anyone, but to end your own pain. Your life was full of love for others and for some sad reason you could not see that the joy you brought far outshined the pain you caused. Oh, I am not unaware of the mistakes you made. It is just that your mistakes usually hurt you more than anyone else.

The whole day yesterday, people recounted ways you helped them out of a bind. Even if you had to "borrow'" from someone else to do it. Guess in some ways we could look at you as a Robin Hood. Friends, family and even a lady with her Australian Shepherd at the park commented on how caring you were. How you approached people with a warm smile and made them feel important. That was your gift, Son, to make everyone feel like they were your favorite. Not just another Joe Blow, but someone you wanted to get to know.

The church was overflowing. They even had to set up a tv to simulcast it in another room for people who wouldn't fit in the sanctuary. There were over 400 people there to celebrate your life. We are going to focus on the love we shared.

If your death can help one person who is suffering with shame from bad choices they have made, it will be worthwhile. This outpouring of love shown to you can show that one person that the pain they cause is insignificant compared to the joy they bring. It is so hard to see the good we do instead of dwelling on the hurts we cause. Ryan, you provided more joy than pain. Everyone, even the worst of the worst, brings joy. If only we could hold on to that.

I will forever miss you, my son. My son, gone from my life too soon. In my heart forever. I just need to close my eyes to see your smile and feel your love.

All my love,
Your beautiful mother

WEDNESDAY, APRIL 14, 2010

Proud Even Now

Cowardly and selfish, that is how I used to feel about anyone who took their own life. I judged them harshly. I applied logic to their final decision. Believing that they sat and analyzed the pain they were going to bring down on their family, friends and the unfortunate person who found the aftermath.

My son's suicide opened my eyes to the truth. Because I know my son would never have done this to hurt me, his daughter or all the people who loved him. He was courageous, not cowardly, and yet he ended his life. Ryan inflicted pain on himself in life, not on others. This final act was not logical, it just was.

God has given me peace about Ryan's final moments on this earth. I will never understand completely the timing of his death, when he seemed to be in such a positive place. That I spoke to him only a couple hours before, and he was making plans confuses me. The death of his Aunt Emma that very morning put sadness in his heart. But the why is left to Ryan and God to understand. It is probably something that Ryan himself could not explain if he was here to answer the question.

What I do know is that drugs and alcohol shortened my son's life. Not only did they shorten his life, they put him through hell on this earth. Ryan never started using substances thinking they would cause him so much pain and rob him of so many possibilities. But they did just that. Drugs and alcohol narrowed his focus when he could have done so much with his talents.

The one thing substance abuse did not rob him of was his loving, generous spirit. Everyone felt like they were Ryan's favorite, and he made people feel so special. His heart reached out to those who suffered the most in life. Eddie was a kid in high school who was burned so badly by his father when he was young that he could not grow hair and had lost both ears. Ryan didn't see his scars. He saw his heart and desperately wanted to be his friend. Eddie and others like him are proof that my son was a brave hero.

My brave hero opened my eyes to my own judgemental heart. People who commit suicide are not selfish or cowardly. Although I still do not understand suicide, I do know that I was mistaken all these years. Now I will grieve my son and ask forgiveness for judging others that chose his same path.

In Him,
Joyful

THURSDAY, APRIL 15, 2010

Today is the Day

"Today is the day!" That is what Mel Fisher said for over a decade while looking for lost treasure. Eventually, after much persistence, he found his

treasure. We all need that attitude in life. Persistence to be the best we can be and to tirelessly pursue our dreams and goals.

Tammy and I have used the example of Mel Fisher's optimistic efforts with our special ed. students for years. I just wish I could give this attitude *to give it your all* to my own children as well as every mother's children. Working hard to achieve your passions is the best way to live. It gives us life.

Drugs and alcohol suck ambition and hope from those who abuse them.

It takes a world of possibilities and shrinks it down to a small room full of hopelessness. I have watched my own children be robbed of the lives they deserve to live. My son lost everything from being a dad to his amazing daughter and even his own life.

I pray that children take the first step away from drugs and toward their passions. Today, some are believing the lies that they shouldn't, and even convince themselves that they are unloveable. Drugs are taking their hope and ambition.

My prayer is that all can believe *"Today is the day"*. The day to put aside the drugs and choose life. Choose to produce and live what they love. Have an enormous world of possibilities and work their butts off to get their reward. Whatever that is.

Today and always in Him,
Joyful and hopeful

FRIDAY, APRIL 16, 2010

His Loss Could Save Lives

Barb,
I wanted to share this earlier, but couldn't get the words written down:

Angels lined the front of the sanctuary as Ryan's life was honored Saturday. "Tell my story." It was Ryan. It was the same as if he had spoken the words. I'm not sure that he didn't because the words were so alive in my heart. Without a doubt, I knew that lives would be saved and enter the Kingdom of God as Ryan's story was told.

A friend sent this to me yesterday. It was so encouraging to read this. And it definitely reflects how I feel about my son's death. Although I would love to ground him or put him in a time out for what he has done, I believe that his death will save others from the same pain. His struggles with drug and alcohol abuse will hopefully snap some addicts out of the pain they are living.

One of my high schoolers who has felt suicidal in the past texted me and said, "Ryan saved my life." She will still need us to walk beside her and let her know how much she is valued. But she sounded hopeful for the first time in a long time. The Bible says be thankful in all things. I am thankful for Ryan in my life. I am thankful for his story being heard by those who need to hear it. Someday, I will be strong enough to be thankful for his death, but not today. Today I am too sad and miss my sweet son too much.

In Him,
Joyful

MONDAY, APRIL 19, 2010

A Rainy Day and a Death Certificate

Thunder, hail, sheets of rain and then a quiet drizzly afternoon. This was the perfect day to be wrapped in a blanket alone on the couch with my thoughts and my pain. There is an ache in my heart as I desperately miss my son, as I copy death certificates to send off to people to prove my son is no longer living.

This simple document, so hard to read with its details of my son's suicide also made me smile. When they asked me for his occupation I decided to go with his heart's desire, so it clearly states Ryan Owen Barber was a CHEF. Now maybe he did not have all the schooling or the paychecks of a chef, but boy, could Ryan come up with amazingly delicious recipes. His goal in life was to feed people his wonderful concoctions, and we all couldn't get enough of his delectable feasts. Somehow he even persuaded me to eat his sushi just once.

Some friends have called, some have stopped by, but today is a chilly, wet day, and I am just being here taking care of details for my son. Still being his mom and helping him out in this small way that I can.

People keep asking how I am doing. Well, not so great. But I bought a pair of rose colored glasses, and I have my family, friends and my faith, so I will get through. My life story includes my son's suicide. It is the truth of my life now. But God is here, right beside me as I send out these death certificates and won't let me go through this alone. Tonight Ron will be home to wrap me in his arms as we miss our precious son together.

God is love, and the one who remains in love remains in God, and God remains in him. (1 John 4:16)

In Him,
Joyful

TUESDAY, APRIL 20, 2010

Brave, I Hope

Bravery or cowardice. Which will it be? Tomorrow I am going back to work to teach my kiddos and see my Mountain Elementary School family. Two weeks and two days after I lost my son by his own hand, through his own pain. I have never been more afraid. This is not a new job. These are people who love me. What am I so afraid of? Me...who am I now? How do I be the one whose son no longer lives among us?

I will get through. I will be brave. Ron has confidence in me. I always tell my kids to be brave and just put one foot in front of the other. Ok, I will try.

There is a staff breakfast at 7:30 before the kids come, so I can see everyone at once. Get it over with. Enjoy the warmth they will give. Then Tammy will be there to get me through with the kids. If I need to step out or run for home she will cover for me like she always does.

So I can do this. I am not a coward. I hope.

In Him,
Joyfully lacking confidence

FRIDAY, APRIL 23, 2010

Going Through the Motions

Sometimes it feels like I am looking in on a life that can't be mine. This reality is like someone else's truth, and I am just going through the motions. When will I wake up and discover it was all a bad dream like the ones I am suffering with every night? Death certificates, ashes of the son I long to touch, simple words that now make me furrow my brow and shake my head. Someone said, "A shotgun wedding," today, and I kept repeating in my head.....shotgun, shotgun, shotgun.

Jenn says live "as if," and I am trying. People keep saying I am brave. Ron and I are brave. What? How would we look if we were not brave? I don't feel brave. I feel sad and numb and scared that I can't live through another moment without our son in this world.

I can't reach my son. I can't sleep or eat. This is not the diet plan I had in mind. By faith, my faith, we will get through. But God knows I am not brave. I am exhausted and sad. My insides are shattered even while I am going through the motions. God, continue to hold me close so I don't stop walking my walk.

In Him,
Joyful

SATURDAY, APRIL 24, 2010

Paul's Encouraging Words

A day with my grandkids got me out of bed and away from my tears. Maybe the exhaustion and enjoyment will help me sleep tonight. Glad I didn't give in to staying in bed with my pain. Tomorrow will be another day to live life.

Paul wrote these encouraging words:
For this reason I bow my knees before the Father, from which every family in heaven and on earth is named. I ask the Father in his great glory to give you the power to be strong inwardly through his spirit. I pray that Christ will live in your hearts by faith and that your life will be in love and be built on love. And I pray that you and all God's holy people will have the power to understand the greatness of Christ's love......how wide and how long and how high and how deep that love is. Christ's love is greater than anyone can ever know, but I pray that you will be able to know that love. Then you can be filled with the fullness of God. With God's power working in us, God can do much, much more than anything we can ask or imagine. To him be glory in the church and in Christ Jesus for all time, forever and ever. Amen. (Ephesians 3: 14-21)
By faith, my faith will see me through this loss and this love.

In Him,
Joyful

FRIDAY, APRIL 30, 2010

A Father's Gift

My kids have a sleepless dad. Ron is staying up all night working on

pictures and videos of our precious son. Each of us is dealing with this suffocating grief in our own ways. His way is to focus on the incredible times we had with Ryan and set aside the fact that we lost him too soon. I pray for my gentle husband's health while he gives us all these visual gifts he is creating out of love for his lost son. The memories in the pictures of Ryan's lasting smile and exuberance for life do take the pain away even while bringing on a flood of tears.

I watch Ron's drive to document the joy Ryan brought to all around him and wish I could pull myself out of bed and away from the tissue box to participate in his creation. Instead I am there to express my gratitude for his cherished videos and to wipe my tears beside this father, my adored husband, whose tears are falling and whose heart is breaking.

This weekend Tanner is joining us to go to Denver and get Ryan's belongings. We will sort through them when we get home and share special items with those who loved Ryan and would treasure a keepsake: a cookbook for David, a fishing hat for Cam, Sublime t-shirts for Natalie and Heather, and the list goes on.

I am most looking forward to the cell phone that may hold pictures my son took of his daughter and himself ice skating or sharing a brief moment cheek to cheek. Last night Ron put together a video of pictures of Ryan that were from the last couple years. My hope is that there will be more pictures on this phone that can make us smile at who he was and how he lived and loved. We will keep the tissues handy and thank God for every captured smile.

In Him,
Joyful yet tear filled

TUESDAY, MAY 4, 2010

Could We Start Again Please from JCSS

Ron and I went to see Jesus Christ Superstar the week after Ryan took his life from us. This song has been stuck in my brain ever since. It just fits how I feel about Ryan's choice to end his life, and how little I understand of God's great plan. The people who walked with Jesus had little understanding of His plans for Christ. Ryan is at peace in his Father's arms, and that is what I need to be comforted with. God gave His son for each of us, even my dear sweet Ryan. The big picture is not for me

to see; mine is just to have faith that God knows. Although I trust God with all that I am, I wish we could start again.

In Him,
Joyful

(Could we start again please?)

MARY MAGDALENE Jesus Christ Superstar

FRIDAY, MAY 7, 2010

Normal to Blog

Desire to write? In the past, I could tell my stress level by how much I was crocheting: no stress-no crocheting, mild stress-crochet like a fiend, high stress-no crocheting. I wish it was the desire to eat that left when I got too much stress.

Now, I am measuring my stress with whether I can write my blog. When my stress was insane I wrote volumes. Now that the stress is more up and down I have to force myself to write.

Stress and grief are fickle. Just when I think I can't take another breath something makes me smile. Then when I seem to be sane, I hear something that sends my heart sinking. Bristly personality comes out of nowhere. A coworker said she was distracted because she had so much on her plate. WHAT? You have a lot on your plate compared to what? I wish I had YOUR problems! Who am I to judge what others are going through? Why do I think I am the only one hurting? I don't want to be this self-centered.

Lisa said we need the minimum of a year to feel normal. That was such an incredible gift. It is okay to not be okay. I am not okay. My life is not okay. I don't want to play. I can't pick up the phone or go out for coffee. I can't sympathize with others or enjoy the park sounds behind my house.

Okay, I will do my life normally again someday, but today I will smile at Ryan's pictures and then cry in Ron's arms. The death of my son is my life now, but it will take time to believe that this reality is the one I am living, not just today, but for all my tomorrows.

In Him,
Joyful at times

TUESDAY, MAY 11, 2010

An Amputation of my Heart

It's like losing an arm or a leg. You will live through it and probably be okay, but you will never be the same. That is what a wise friend told me about my son, Ryan's, suicide.

This was a great illustration because we have a friend who lost his leg in a motorcycle accident. We have watched him at church progress from the hospital, to a wheelchair, to a walker, to crutches, to walking unassisted with his prosthetic. He is living with his injury, but his life will never be what it was. There will be blessings that come and hardships to bear. With faith, friends and family he will get through the rest of his life with one leg and one prosthetic. Life may be better than it was, but it will never be the same as it was. I had a coworker advise me to just be normal, have a normal day. Choose to be happy. What? Life is not normal. I am not happy. It is not as it was before Ryan's death. Through my faith I know I will be okay. But I need to walk through this as my friend did with his amputation and find my legs slowly. Today I am not okay that my son is gone, that I will never pick up the phone and hear him say, "Hello, Beautiful!" Ryan will never wow me with his latest pizza crust recipe again. This is a new reality in my life and the lives of all touched by his amazingly generous heart.

It has been a month. I am not even in that wheelchair yet. First, I need to recover from the shock and reality that is my son's suicide. Then I will begin the process of moving toward standing on my feet again.

I admire Maurice's courage and persistence to walk on his own. His recovery will be an example for my own recovery. The unexpected path that each of us finds ourselves on was not by choice. It was swift and tragic. Yes, I will have normal days eventually. But today, I am still on my

knees with pain. Even if you cannot see the amputation in my heart as I miss and mourn my son, it is as real as my friend's. Through this I need to be as honest with myself as I am with others about how I am. Of course, there are moments when I am okay. But overall it is going to take time and all your prayers so I can heal from what is now a part of my life story.

In Him,

Joyful

FRIDAY, MAY 14, 2010

Smile on My Hand, Love on His Arm

Write SMILE on your hands and LOVE on your arm. Tanner got a tattoo of a fly rod with Rest In Peace Ryan on his right forearm. He misses his brother and felt an urgency to get this tribute on his arm forevermore. I wrote SMILE on the palms of my hands to remind myself to smile. I always believed I could smile through anything in the halls of my elementary school that is filled with children I love. Not so much smiling lately though.

It says in the Bible to be thankful in all things. That too has been tough for me. Then today a friend was sharing about the struggles of her child at age 40. Her beloved daughter is still battling the horrors of drug and alcohol abuse. I was thankful in that moment. As much as I will miss my son, I would not want to watch him agonize with the addictions that haunted him for another 16 years. Ryan loved so much of life, but could not quite get control enough of his substance abuse to be the man he longed to be. Perhaps the biggest ache in his heart was that he was not "manning up" to be the dad he wanted Lis to have in her life.

Suicide is never the answer. It takes away all hope of recovery. But since Ryan chose this path, I must find peace in his decision to stop the pain. Only a few hours before Ryan took his life, he told me on the phone not to worry about his sister, his brothers or him. He assured me that they would all be okay. "Mom, you pray for us, so have faith!" Finally, I believe him. He is okay. God's arms have a greater reach than mine. God has all of us in His arms, protected from what life challenges us with. I do believe!

I thank God that Ryan was able to spend the best week of his life with his daughter in January this year. They went ice skating, swimming and just hung out together. Ryan was able to be completely present with his adorable little girl that entire week. She was his total focus, and he was hers. Natalie and Ron both commented on the agony Ryan and Lis went through when the time came to part at the end of their time together. Each had created an amazing, fresh bond with the other that week. Neither knew this would be their last time together, but God must have known and blessed them with this incredible gift.

I thank God that each of us is in His loving care. I pray that when the time comes to hold my son again I will be able to thank God in person.

In Him,
Joyful

SATURDAY, MAY 15, 2010

Heart Rocks That Touch My Heart

"This is for you." Ryan was four when he found me my first heart rock. From then on all four of my munchkins would share their discoveries of heart rocks with me. My collection is quite extensive. I always called my kids my hearts. Even the family ring on my finger has a heart for each of my kids, Ron and me. The heart rocks led to us finding the perfect rock on each of our incredible trips. We have rocks in our yard from the Arctic Circle, Key West and of course an array of rocks from the beautiful southwest.

One of my helpful fifth grade students loves to clean my teacher's desk. Last week, she was sharpening all the pencils from the crock that holds them on my desk. She found a perfect red heart rock in the bottom. It brought a smile to my face and a tear to my eye as I remembered Ryan getting off a plane. He gave each of us a hug. Then he reached into the pocket of his oversized shorts and handed me this heart rock. "Look Mom, I think it is the best one yet!" I think he was right.

My sweet friend found me a heart rock that was perfect this week. The rock was amazing, but her sweet, loving heart was what touched mine. Here I thought I might never receive another one, and now I know that my collection is just getting started.

In Him,
Joyful

THURSDAY, MAY 20, 2010

Retirement Party, Bad Idea

So dumb! Today I didn't listen to my gut and went to a retirement party that I knew would be too much. It was filled with people who have poured into my son and people whose kids I have been able to pour into. A park full of educators who all are exhausted as the end of the year barrels toward us. A few moments out of our busyness of report cards, packing up classrooms and getting in that one last math skill that the kiddos didn't quite grasp.

My mistake was not wearing a sign that said, "Don't talk to me or ask me how I am." Not that I could have handled just standing there alone either. Today I decided I don't want to play this life this way. It is time for a do over. Back to Spring Break. I will go up, get Ryan and bring him down for Easter and my birthday. Time to rewrite the script. Where is the editor? We definitely need a rewrite.

These people care. I care about them too. But I just want to run and crawl under my bed and pout. Today is not the day to be social or buck up or act "as if". Today is the day that the flood is back, and I definitely need more Kleenex.

To all who love me, thanks for your prayers and your love. I really am grateful even as I am running for the car.

In Him,
Joyfully Hanging On By a Thread

SUNDAY, MAY 23, 2010

My Bed Can't Be My Life

But I want to write. I think I need to write, so why am I not writing? I even had a wonderful weekend doing yard work with my hubby and girls that I love. What a good feeling to look out at our accomplishment. Then off camping with Ron, the grandkids and the rest of our family. I should be tired but pleasantly so. Things to write about? Indeed, life is moving forward every day.

I just feel stuck. Like I don't want to move. Anything and everything is overwhelming. A night out with a dear friend who made me a wonderful dinner, a sweet movie and hot tub with deep conversation seemed a chore. Nothing about the night was not great except my heart. Going places and participating is healthy, but I just want to hide. Crawl into bed and sleep; yes please. Then when I go to bed, sleep doesn't come anyway.

This grief process is tough. Thankfully those I love are not allowing me to isolate, and they are encouraging me to write. I need this blog, and I need you to help me when I get stuck. Ron is so patient, loving and encouraging. I thank God we are clinging to each other through this process. Missing Ryan is good. He mattered, and we shared our lives with him. That is something else I thank God for. The opportunity to have our chosen family of six.

Camping in our 1975 yellow van brought back such warm memories of trips with all the kids. Having our granddaughters up in the top bunk

gave me hope for the future. We will just have to go on without our
Scooter. For now, I need to just take it one day at a time.
In Him,

Joyful

THURSDAY, MAY 27, 2010

Honesty is the Way to Go

Keep thinking the tears will be less and the smiles more. But the tears
just keep flowing. I don't think I have ever been more honest about my
feelings before in my life. Sadness envelopes my heart, and I just admit
this loneliness to myself. I thank God for my friends and my family and

that I am really not alone. God is kind to me even through all of this heartache. I am so glad I don't walk through this alone.

There have been other tragedies in my life. In the past I have tried to pretend I was tough enough, brave enough, strong enough. Why? Others saw my pain even when I tried to protect them from it. If I have learned anything from my son, it was to be honest and let others see what I am going through. Then they will be honest and reach out for my help when they need it. Let's admit we are shaken when life throws sorrow our way, and then we can all be there for each other through the hard times that are bound to come.

In Him,
Joyful but not alone

FRIDAY, MAY 28, 2010

Gordon's Concerts

Our hometown has a duck pond surrounded by sloping grass banks at the center of town. What is outstanding in our town is that Russell Gordon started putting on Friday night concerts all summer over twenty years ago. So on Friday nights you can find the young and the old in our town dancing, sitting and chatting in lawn chairs or just strolling around catching up with each other.

I love the concerts, the people, all the freedom kids have and oh yeah, the music. Tonight we went to our first concert of the season. So many friends, kids coming up for a hug. Russ dedicated the entire summer series to Ryan and a couple others who have left this earth but not our hearts. It meant the world to Ron and me to see Ryan honored by this man who is our friend and has such a heart for music and our town.

Although my eyes sprung a few leaks as we wandered around listening to great music and hugging friends, I am glad I mustered the courage to attend. Ron draws strength from talking to loved ones about Ry. I find that my tears flow, and I can't quite catch my breath. Thankfully, as we walked around the pond hand in hand, we were both loving each other right where we are on this path without our son.

It does bring a smile remembering how he loved these concerts from the time he was four. Boy, did he have fun dancing with all the pretty little girls! Hope this summer we can take our grandkids out to dance and enjoy the concerts at the pond.

In Him,
Joyfully embraced by our hometown

SATURDAY, JUNE 5, 2010

Saturday, Two Months Later

Two months ago our lives were changed forever by Ryan's decision to take his life. Today we are still aching with the reality of his passing out of our lives and into his Father's kingdom. Through these two months God has walked beside us every step. His faithfulness should be proof that none of us ever has to travel through this life on our own. Through times when we find ourselves on our knees with the pains of life and through the times we celebrate the fruits of life, God is faithfully at our side. Even those days where life just unfolds into kind of a "just another day" kind of day we need to remember that we are not alone.

Today was a day full of mixed emotions. Grandkids in the morning, struggling to adjust to our independent daughter being home, community Summerfest filled with people we love and share our lives with, and the struggles to realize our son will never share this life again.

Thank God for reminding us that time will bring us all together in a different place. A place without the mixed emotions and pressures of this life waits in our future. The hurts are real and the ache is deep, but His presence with us keeps us taking the next step forward.

In Him,
Joyful

MONDAY, JUNE 14, 2010

A Mother's Protection is Limited

Shaken up! Natalie was just in an earthquake in San Diego. Everyone at camp is fine, and they ended up having an amazing "Cross Talk" out in the field. My daughter's courage astounds me. She was a part of a "Cardboard Confession" where each person puts a life problem on one side of a piece of cardboard and God's solution on the other. Natalie put, "My brother committed suicide two months ago" on one side, and "God's grace and presence are getting me through" on the other. Powerful, courageous, intimate, incredible. God is using her loss to reach others. Natalie had spent the week with these middle schoolers coming into the gift store to have her make them smoothies. So they were familiar with her face but not her pain.

Who was sitting on that field after hearing God's sacrifice on the cross and made more vulnerable by an earthquake shaking things up? God knows just who was there, and who needed to hear each Cardboard Confession. Reaching others by openly sharing our pain is giving God a longer reach. Letting Him touch others with our loss and the loving life our son led while we were blessed to have him with us. Ryan died too early, all of us will agree, but God will draw us near to Him through our sorrow and pain.

I thank God for His incredible love for my children. My protection can't stand up to an earthquake or a shotgun, but He has each of them in His embrace. His love for each of them out-measures even my mother's heart.

God, thank you for the time I had with Ryan and the joy he brought into my life. Help me to be grateful for every moment I have with my other children, grandchildren and all those I love in this life. Thank you also for the hope that I have to be reunited with those who are gone in heaven. Be thankful in all things you say. Okay, I am thankful today that Natalie and the campers are okay. I am thankful that Ryan is in your presence, and that I told him a million times how much I loved him.

In Him,
Joyful

FRIDAY, JUNE 18, 2010

Pawn Shop Tears

Pawn shops are unsafe places for me right now. I didn't have a clue until yesterday that this is the reality. Cathy and I went into one to look for an amplifier for her son. When she said she was going to stop and look at the guns, I looked up. There was a wall filled with rifles and shotguns and cases with handguns. I crumbled into a sobbing mass.

Today I am taking a self-induced time out. Lissa is up with Cam's family rock climbing, Ron is off chasing shadows for the Solstice, and I am resting and spending time with myself. No big revelations other than the fact that I am incapable of taking naps. Oh yes, and I am jealous of people who can take naps.

Reflecting, contemplating, meditating. These are all words I could use to describe my afternoon. But if I am honest, I just needed to lay on my bed and veg out with online tv shows and Redbox movies. I learned that it is not nice to shoot a goat in the leg, and Monk has too many issues to enjoy going camping. So I have had my spell of laziness and don't feel any better for it. Guess I should have gone to the Gordon's Concert after all. Ron is probably right that being around others is healing. It will be nice when I am enjoying being social again.

In Him,

Joyful

SATURDAY, JUNE 19, 2010

First Father's Day Without Her Daddy

Her fifth Father's Day is her first Father's Day without her daddy. We are all grieving the loss of our Ryan, but little Lissa will never have another daddy to take her ice skating or tuck her in at night. I thank God she had that marvelous week with him this past January. They were inseparable and laughed and hugged continuously. Although he was not able to live with his little girl, she was the light of his life. The pain of not spending Halloween with her led him to take a suicidal picture in October. Spending Easter apart was obviously more than he could bear. Ryan had a lot of love for all the special people in his life and never met a stranger. But the great love of his life was this adorable, blonde haired, brown eyed little five year old.

She is having trouble getting to sleep at night. She just sobs for her daddy. Her love for him is as great as his love for her. I thank God that I am able to gaze into her precious brown eyes that are so like her dad's.

Tomorrow will not be too difficult for Lis. She doesn't really understand that this day should be about her dad and her. Father was not a word that she used for her daddy. Future Father's Days will be more difficult to live through as she grows and becomes more aware of her loss.

I pray that those of us around Lis can convince her that Ryan never meant to leave her even though his actions tell a different story. His love for her and his distance from her because of addictions were more than he could take. Loneliness for his incredible daughter broke his heart on that awful night. Hopefully, his great love for her will be of some comfort as she grows up with the sad reality of how she lost her one and only daddy.

In Him,

Joyful

THURSDAY, JUNE 24, 2010

An Almost Six Year Old Disciple For Christ

Beautiful smiles all the way into their identical, brillliant, brown eyes. Lis and I went to Santa Fe today to get reprints of the last picture of her and her daddy. This precious picture was taken of them at the ice skating rink in January. The odd thing is we didn't go with them to the rink. Ry was taking pics on his phone which he broke and there was no sd card. So the million dollar question is where did this now-so-important-to-us picture come from? Lis attached a #1 Dad ribbon to it that she got on Father's Day at church. So off we went to make a bazillion copies so we can share them with everyone, and so we never accidentally lose this important treasure.

His eyes and her eyes are fully content in this frame. Just spending time with each other is the greatest, and it is evident in both of their so similar eyes.

Lis felt the need to share her loss with the guy at Walgreens who helped us copy the picture and the lady sweeping the floors at KFC, who by the way, lost her daughter a decade ago and is still grieving. Both of their reactions were the same to this adorable almost six year old. Tears filled their eyes as compassion gripped their hearts, and they both gave her a quick, ok even though I am a stranger, hug. She is a witness as she shares her love and loss with others boldly. Then she told them that her daddy was in heaven with Jesus, and he was safe and happy. I know they both believed her, and as they went on with their daily tasks their lives were changed. I can imagine them sharing with coworkers and maybe something will remind them as they arrive home, and then they will relate her story to their own loved ones.

Oh, Christ, how You can use the heart of a sweet little girl to pass your love and message innocently to others. She is just as bold about sharing her simple little prayer that she proudly sings and others desperately need.

Lord above, comfort me.
Give me courage. Help me see.
Guide my actions. Guide my words.
Let me know my prayers are heard.
Amen

To break it down, it is a simple prayer, but Jesus was a simple man. So it is not just enough for each of us. It is perfect for each of us. We all need comfort and courage to get through the heartbreaks of life, no matter how big or how small. Guidance for our actions and our words is key to living a guilt free, fulfilling life. Knowing our prayers are heard gives us the promise that God is always walking beside us if we just stop and take hold of His hand.

A few Sundays back, Pastor Shawn had each of us hold up our arms like a toddler does to his daddy when he wants to be picked up. What Shawn pointed out was a powerful illustration of God's loving us as His children. At times, when our little ones reach up their arms to us we gently pick them up and snuggle their fears away. Other times He, like fathers on this earth, let His children walk on their own.

Grandkids in Papa's hammock

Not alone, just on their own two feet they walk beside Him to build their strength.

At times we need comfort. At times we

need courage. Either way we are safe in His loving embrace. Whether He is carrying us through or merely holding our hand and guiding us along, He is getting us through with His constant presence in our lives.

In Him,
Joyful

TUESDAY, JUNE 29, 2010

My Daddy by Lissa

A great big box is sitting in our driveway. Dorothy lovingly packed up some of Ry's things and gave them to us last weekend. Lis wanted to dig through the boxes all by herself. She kept running in the house to show me his fishing backpack, fishing vest and waders. It was already crystal clear to her who should get what from her daddy's box. Uncle Cam could have the Powerbait, but the Corona flip flops she would keep till her feet got big enough. She carefully carried in a suede vest that had once belonged to my dad. I explained that her dad had been honored when my mom gave him clothes that my dad had worn. She immediately started a pile for her future little boy. This task was incredibly important to my purposeful granddaughter. Her face showed clearly how serious she took the task of selecting just the right treasure to save for each person. After she had sorted through everything, she told me she needed to make a list about her daddy so she wouldn't forget. So here goes........

I love my daddy.
He loves me.

He knows how I am doing.

He knows I am a good girl.

I liked going shopping and ice skating and the movies and just being silly together.

He was very silly when he was a little boy.

He keeps me so warm whenever he hugs me.

He keeps me safe.

He has me in his hands.

He knows how hard I try on my homework.

We liked to play some games together.

We played at the park together.

I liked hearing about him and Uncle Tanner playing homeless in clown suits.

My daddy was so smart, so I am so smart.

I have the same eyes as him.

When he smiled at me it made me happy.

I miss going places with him.

I miss his smile.

I miss him hugging me and cuddling with me.

I miss him playing games with me.

He won't sing songs with me anymore.

I miss him loving me here, but he does love me in heaven.

But he had to die because he fell asleep and woke up dead in heaven with Jesus. And that is all about my daddy. Lissa

In Him,
Joyful

FRIDAY, JULY 2, 2010

Let Freedom Write

Freedom, Freedom, Freedom. No, I am not talking about America's freedom, although this is certainly the weekend to celebrate that and all who have made our freedom possible. Freedom came for a visit tonight. This incredible young lady is the one who blessed us with the poem for Ryan's goodbye party handouts. What an amazing young mother she has become. I remember her proudly sitting behind the counter at the eye doctor's office when she got one of her first jobs. She was so mature and responsible even then. Well, at least that is how I saw her.

Ron and I had a wonderful visit with her, and she was full of wisdom, comfort and understanding. This knowing young lady was one of Ryan's closest friends and knew so much about his generous heart. How he made everyone in the room feel like they got the most of his attention, and each felt they were his absolute favorite. It was just Ry's gift. That ornery little smile that crept all the way up into his eyes. Somehow he just made us all feel like we were in on whatever scheme he was cooking up. Freedom can know for sure from his insightful mom that she truly was one of his most cherished friends.

I know it is her poem, but I need to beg forgiveness and share it here for those who did not get a card at the service. It is perfectly written, each and every word is just right. What a blessing it has been for us all to have this pearl to remember Ryan with and to know that he is safe in God's garden.

I was walking in a garden as the sunshine kissed my face
And I stared in pure amazement at the beauty of this place.
The painted sky of greens and blues took my breath away
Like someone mixed a sunset, with the Milky Way.
There were a hundred kinds of plants in different shades of green
Some to me, familiar, but most I'd never seen.
Flowers by the thousands went as far as I could see
Inside this sweet nirvana I felt completely free.
I heard a voice behind me say, "I call this garden Zion"
I didn't have to turn around to know that it was Ryan.
With a quiver in my footstep and my voice caught in my chest
I turned to see him standing there looking more than best.
With a glow of light around him and no sadness in his eyes

I didn't know quite what to say, so I began to cry.

He took me by the hand and said, "You don't need to shed more tears.

For every drop my friends have cried, have made this garden here.

Don't dwell upon the how's and why's that led me to this place,

But rest assured in knowing that I'm engulfed by God's grace.

Inside this serene garden there is no sadness and no pain,

I don't feel any darkness and I don't feel any shame.

There is only peace and comfort that I feel inside my soul

For inside Heaven's Garden the hurt no longer takes its toll.

So thank you for your teardrops and I know that it's been rough

But I no longer need the salty rain, this garden's big enough."

Written by: Freedom Spencer Elliott 4-10-10 Absolutely perfect, Freedom. Thank you for this precious image of Ryan, peaceful forevermore.

In Him,

Joyful

SATURDAY, JULY 3, 2010

I am Okay More Now

Driving home from running errands I had a moment of panic. It had been a busy day, and I had been okay. Monday will be only three months since we lost Ryan, and I had an okay day. How can that be? I felt so guilty, like did he matter so little that I can just move past the pain of his loss and go about my life without him so easily? It just tore my mother's heart.

When I put my tears away and wiped up with the now ever close-by tissues, I realized that it is not disloyal to have okay moments or even okay days. Ryan is gone. I miss him desperately and wish life had turned out differently for him and for all of us. But life will continue to unfold day by day, moment by moment. My love for him and my broken heart for his loss are real even when I am not dwelling on him.

A month ago people would ask me how I was doing. My pat answer to their question was, "Hanging in". I couldn't bring myself to lie and say, "Okay". Now I find myself responding with an ok most of the time and meaning it. There are still plenty of just hanging in moments and times when I can't stop crying, but the normal moments are returning to life. Guess I need to feel thankful for those times and not guilty about the healing.

In Him,

Joyful

THURSDAY, JULY 8, 2010

Others, Not Me, Me, Me

Hypocrite. Yep, that is an accurate term to describe me. I preach the **"Others"** speech to students and anyone who will listen. Reach out to others, help others, the harder your life is the more you should focus outward on others. That is not what I have been doing these past three months.

I chose not to take middle schoolers to camp. I have not been calling and hanging out with kids or my friends. I have been spending way too much time in my bed and in my sorrow. I have turned inward, exactly what I warn others not to do. Reach out? Not now. I am too sad, too broken, too scared, too overwhelmed. These are my excuses to not reach out or even live life.

Okay, so I have a lot of anguish in my life right now. Ryan is dead at his own hand. Natalie is trying desperately to find her direction in life with all the turmoil she has had to endure. Elissa is with us, but no guarantees for how long. Tanner is off making his way, and I barely see him. Cameron and Brittney have their hands full with work, kids and church.

Dorothy is back in Flagstaff adjusting to life without Ryan. So I have ample excuses to take to my bed. Time to count my woes instead of my blessings. Right!?

No, that is not the way it is supposed to work. These past three months, like the rest of my life, have been chocked full of incredible blessings. I have reconnected with so many friends. I have a much clearer picture of who my son was to countless people in his short, twenty-four year life. My family and friends have been here if I would only reach out and accept their love and support. It has been my poor choice to walk away and turn away from my life. This is all in my control. I need to be a part of others' lives. It is who I am, and it is what I do. No one advised me to stop being me because life got hard, but that is what I have been doing. Instead of drawing strength from being there for others, I have decided to be a hermit.

That may be the way to go for a crab, but not for me. So tomorrow is a new day, the start of a new week. So call me and get me off my mattress and out in the world with OTHERS!

In Him,

Joyful

TUESDAY, JULY 13, 2010

Daddy Sang Me Happy Birthday From Heaven

He should have been here! Lissa will just have to have her birthdays and other special days without him. We are going to take her to Disneyland this weekend and to the beach. Oh, how I wish he was here to see her smiles. It is one of those days when I just can't understand how he chose to leave her and all of us behind.

Ron said we will take his ashes and toss some in the ocean where he once enjoyed surfing. Okay, that is nice I guess, but really, not so much! I don't want to take Ry's ashes to California. I want to take Ry to California. It's not even close to being okay with me that he is not going to crack jokes and call me beautiful. That his delightful daughter won't have him to teach her to be kind to all the people at the park and in life.

I am definitely wallowing in a pity party tonight. It is not okay for me, his mom, but I had twenty-four years with him. This sweet angel didn't even get six years with him. Even when he was here he wasn't there for her most of the time. I think this was one of the hardest things for him in his life and in his addictions. Not being there for his precious daughter. Ryan ached that he was not there for all those he loved. He was always more disappointed in himself than any of us were.

The loss of his life, his absence from our lives seems so unnecessary. I just pray that others can make a different choice and realize that the best way out of any situation, no matter how difficult, is to just keep moving through. Life has highs and lows for everyone. Some have a harder time than others, but life always cycles through, and things never stay horrible forever. There are always better times ahead. We just have to stick around to experience them.

So it has obviously been a long bittersweet day. All four of my grandkids were here enjoying each other. Boy, did Timmy love his cupcake and ice cream! Now as it is getting late Lis is sitting here building with her new GIRL Legos. She just looked over and saw the fresh tears in my eyes. We talked a bit about her daddy. In all her six year old wisdom, she told me not to be sad. "Daddy is up in heaven with Jesus, and Noni, he sang

'Happy Birthday' in heaven to me this morning. He misses being here for my birthday, but he needs to be there, and it is okay."

Simplifying is key. I believe Ry is in heaven. I believe he is at peace. I just selfishly want him here with us. But I will get through. Her hugs and simple logic help me more than she could know.

In Him,
Joyful

FRIDAY, JULY 30, 2010

Unfortunately, Now Our Loss is Their Loss Too

Rainy day, thunder and lightning. An amazing display just for us to enjoy while God helps us out with the water bill. Ron and I are clinging to each other in the downpour as we learned of another young man taken too early from our little town. This twenty-one year old was in our cub scout troop, and when Natalie was in the first grade she was convinced she would marry him someday. His parents helped with the boy scout popcorn sale and were always there with his little sister to lend a hand when needed.

My wish was that our loss could cover it for the whole town and no other family would have to experience the loss of their child or brother. Here is what I think: When this family found out about Ryan's death they were so sad for us and prayed for us. Before Ryan died, we were so saddened by the loss of two of our kids' close friends and felt so bad for their devastated families. Our hearts grieved for their loss completely unaware that soon we would be walking in their shoes. Today, there is another family in our little town trying to wrap their hearts and heads around the news that their hopes and dreams for their son are shattered. His little sister will never get to be an aunt to his little ones or have him dance with her at her wedding.

So this family will need to be supported by this generous community as we were and we will all pray that our town has lost enough of our twenty something kiddos for a very long time. Even in this close knit community there is loss. The gift of a small town is that we are a part of each other's lives and come together to surround each other.

In Him,
Joyful

THURSDAY, AUGUST 5, 2010

No Other Mother

No other mother! Today, Ron and I went to the funeral of a twenty-one year old that was in our cub scout troop. His life ended way too soon just like Ryan's. This is too much. Our little town has lost too many wonderful, young people in the past couple years. The kids are weary of the constant grief and the worrying about who is next. Tanner has lost more friends and family at twenty-three years old than I have lost in my fifty-four years.

We discussed it in the car on the way to the graveside service. Ron and I don't need any more members of the Parents Who Have Lost Children group. These wonderful people were just feeling compassion for us a few short months ago, and now they are burying their beloved son. This is definitely not how the world is supposed to work. Our kids are supposed to bury us when they are much older themselves, preferably with grandkids of their own.

This young man was in the Army, and so at the graveside service they had a twenty-one gun salute. I knew it was coming but was totally unprepared for my reaction to the deafening gunshot sounds. My whole body drooped. It was as if Ryan had shot himself dead right in that horrifying moment. I was crushed. If a dear, young man had not put his arm around me and lifted me up, I might have fallen to the ground at that terrifying instant.

No mother, father, sister, brother or friend should have to suffer the loss of those they love. Today was exactly four months since Ryan shot himself. It would have been a difficult day no matter what. Watching a mom cling to the casket of her only son made it almost impossible to bear.

In Him,
Joyful

WEDNESDAY, AUGUST 11, 2010

Terrified of Friends?

Just when I catch myself having a normal day, I gasp at the thought that Ryan is forever gone, and I am just living my life as if he is in Colorado and could call any day. I have read the books and know I am right on target with the grief process, but oh, how clinical that seems. This is my son that is gone, my twenty-four year old son, Lissa's daddy, my kids' brother. He is never going to cook for us again, never call or torment us with his funny humor. Life must go on. I know it must, but how can the sun shine and the birds sing when our hearts ache with the pain of this loss?

At times, I feel like I am betraying his memory by laughing with friends, playing with my grandkids or even watching TV. A friend asked me the other day if I wanted to watch a movie. I have not been able to focus on a movie in these last four months. It seems overwhelming to even think of sitting through a movie. So there are good days and bad now, four months out from the senseless loss of my son.

Tomorrow terrifies me. The new school year begins with all district employees together for a meet and greet kickoff to the year. Ryan's former teachers will be there. People who adored my ornery, little booger. My friends promise to surround me and keep me safe. Why do I feel so timid and afraid of seeing people who touched my life and his in a most positive way? I don't understand my feelings, but tonight I can't stop crying, and I feel mortified just thinking of being in such a big crowd. These people would never hurt me, and I am ashamed of my fears.

Pray for me to find the courage and strength to make it through tomorrow and all the days that will come after tomorrow.

In Him,
Joyful

Beautiful support family at my Mom's service

THURSDAY, AUGUST 12, 2010

My Oxygen Mask First

Cooperation, working together, is a little song they sing on Sesame Street. It is an important lesson we begin learning when we are young and should continue working on well into old age. People who help other people and who work at being positive rather than negative are much happier than those who turn away and grumble about life.

Today at school we had an amazing speaker, Nate Ecklund, who reminded us of how important cooperating and encouraging each other is for the adults as well as the children in a school or any workplace.

The one thing he said that really sticks with me is that we need to take care of ourselves first in order to fully be available to others. He reminded us that when in an airplane we learn to place the oxygen mask over our own face in a crisis before assisting a child. In a real emergency or rough time we tend to take care of others and forget that taking care of ourselves is the first lesson. We need the oxygen to fully assist others. Likewise, we need to be honest with ourselves about our needs before we can take care of others' needs.

This has been an important lesson for me. I tend to turn outward to avoid dealing with my own pains. It is a coping mechanism that eventually catches up with me when I completely deplete my emotional reserves. Today was extremely hard for me. But I put on my oxygen mask, and let those who love me take care of me. I set the stage to be able to handle a difficult day in a way that allowed me to make it through. Many tears later, I can honestly say that I am glad I didn't bail at the Meet and Greets of this new school year. So now, though I am emotionally exhausted, I know I took the next step in my grieving process.

In Him,

Joyful

WEDNESDAY, AUGUST 18, 2010

Heart Rocks from Heart Kids

Ryan found me heart rocks ever since he was four years old. Since his death, so many others have blessed me with more heart rocks to add to my most treasured collection. These amazing people are so much more a treasure in my life than even the perfect heart rocks they find and share.

God has gifted me with a life filled with heart people who love me, and who I would never want to live without. Losing Ryan has been hard. Hard on all of us, because Ryan was a gatherer of more precious stones than the heart shaped ones. He gathered people's hearts with his kindness and attention to their needs. I thank God my son was that person who put others before himself and generously shared his life, although short, with us.

When Ry got off the airplane the last time I saw him, he reached in his pocket and pulled out a heart rock he had been carrying around just for me. The rock was not the gift. The gift was his caring enough to carry it around till he could give it to me.

Tomorrow I begin a new school year. This year, like years in the past, I fully intend to gather "heart kids". Kids who will steal my heart and hopefully learn from me that not only are they bright and beautiful, but they are also valued for just who they are. Ry was not the easiest student starting all the way back in preschool. But there are teachers who poured their love into my son with their incredibly selfless hearts.

So test scores and best teaching practices for reading aside, I am a teacher of heart kids, and I hope to teach them more than test questions. I hope to show them that they matter. Gathering heart kids for a lifetime is my biggest reward.   In Him, *Joyful*

FRIDAY, AUGUST 20, 2010

Not So Funny Pranks

Alcohol and drugs. If we could only find a way to eliminate the abuse of these two demons, so much pain would be saved. Today TMan finally went to court for his poor choice so many months ago when he ended up spending Superbowl Sunday in the slammer. His bright idea the night before, after too many drinks, was to enter a hotel swimming pool and arrange the patio furniture neatly in the bottom of the pool. A barrel of laughs till the cops showed up. A few years prior he took a joy ride in a golf cart when he was sober. Imagine the shock of finding out these were both felonies. No real victims, no harm, no foul. Not at all the way the courts saw his shenanigans.

So today he pleaded guilty to a fourth degree felony and will have it all erased when his years' probation are up. But the lesson we learned was not so much in T's case. The court was filled with those in the jail's custody and those who were headed there. We witnessed young and not so young who had real victims in their stupid drunken and drug induced crimes.

Oh trust me, there were plenty of excuses and even more promises to make better choices in the future. But you know, as a nervous observer, I wasn't believing much of what they said any more than the judge was. There was not a lot of hope in that room full of addicts. Of course, most of them would not recognize their addictions.

Today was sad, for my son in court, for my son gone too soon, for all those who are paying for crimes, for all their victims. Mostly today was sad because there didn't seem to be a solution of hope that would stop the endless parade through the courtroom in our town or in towns all across our country. No one expects drugs or alcohol to become a huge problem in their life. It is just meant to be good fun among friends, until it is not.
In Him,
Joyful, wanting to be hopeful

TUESDAY, AUGUST 24, 2010

Blogging and Blubbering

I had a horrible dream last night and couldn't get back to sleep. Finally I had to get up and make sure Natalie was okay. Just to see her breathing would have been enough, but I am grateful she woke up, and I could give her a hug and tell her how much she means to me. I just can't bear the thought of losing another of my children. It is not okay that Ry is gone, but how could I live through losing another one of my precious babies?

When I tell friends that I am terrified of another tragic loss, they comfort me and say that won't happen. Unfortunately, the statistics don't agree. Family members are more likely to commit suicide when they have someone close to them leave so suddenly at their own hand. I am not dwelling on that though. Most of the time I am not focusing on it.

Cameron, Tanner and Natalie are so broken from the loss of their brother. It is hard for any of us to wrap our brains around this truth. People are quite sensitive to Ron's and my pain, but the kids' friends don't feel comfortable talking so much. Because of that, they have not had the same opportunities to process with others.

The grief path is different for each of us, and we just need to be honest with each other and those who love us about what we need from them. Today, I needed to hug Natalie and know she is as okay as she can be with the pain in her life. At work, I was blessed with a quiet day of IEP folders and schedules, so I had time to sit and grieve with a full box of tissues and several friends who came by at just the right time.

It is still hard for me to socialize. Harder still to pick up the phone and make a plan. I need each of my friends in my life but can't quite push through to set up the much needed times with them. My bed is not my life, but I still reside there way too much. It calls to me as I battle emotional exhaustion. I know I need to start walking, and Kylie would love it. But I plan to and then don't. Someday soon. This is a journey, a tunnel to move through, they say. And they should know I guess.

In Him,
Joyfully and honestly blubbering

WEDNESDAY, AUGUST 25, 2010

Others, Honestly

Others. I started this blog with that idea. Others. When the going gets tough, don't turn yourself inward and wallow in self pity. Reach out to others and make a difference. Boy, was that easier before April 5th! Ryan's suicide has rocked my world but not my faith. But it has also made me realize that being honest and truthful about what you can and cannot handle is the best way through. So, although I have probably been there for others in some ways, mostly I have had to step back and take care of me. Sometimes, letting others take care of us is the honest and right course to take.

Time is healing the constant ache. Nothing will fix the hole in our family that Ryan's death has left. He was our guy who called everyone just to say, "Hey, Beautiful, have a great day!" Ryan will forever be missed, but our lives will go on without his precious presence in them.

Now, God may be calling on me to reach out to another mother with a tragically, broken heart. Our friend's son took his life a few weeks ago and shattered his family. His mother called yesterday and wanted to get together to talk. I have not been brave enough to listen to her message, so Tillie just told me about it. Tonight I am praying for the strength to call her back. I will have to take it step by step to see how I can handle my pain and hers. *I*

can do all things through God who strengthens me. Now I just have to lay my heart and my fears on Him and believe.

Pray for me and I will pray for you. That is how we make it through, together in Christ.

In Him,
Joyfully healing

MONDAY, AUGUST 30, 2010

Amber's Precious Poems

The love of an eleven year old for her cousin. This is a beautiful glimpse into her thoughts, understanding and heartache over the death of a cousin who always made her feel special. What a sweet gift she is.

Hey aunt barb! its amber here is the poem you wanted that i wrote at nana's house. And i also am giving you another poem i wrote on the way home

I don't understand?!

He knew

He knew more than thousands of people loved him

Why would he do this?

To lis

To himself

To everyone

It doesn't seem real! but i know

Ryan didn't kill himself

I wanted to go

Run away

It didn't seem real

It still doesn't!

I still cry when i hear the song "my son"

And natalie with me in arizona

i love you aunt barb!

WEDNESDAY, SEPTEMBER 1, 2010

"I Will Carry You in and Give You Life"

Christ's love for me, for you, for us. He was willing to take our sin on his pure life to give us the hope of being with Him for eternity. ("By Your Side" by Tenth Avenue North)

What do I have to do to earn this incredible gift? Believe. That's it. I don't have to do good works, although His love makes me want to. I don't have to pray, although His love makes me want to spend so much time in communication with Him. I don't have to be perfect, because He was perfect for me. I just have to believe.

God has made the perfect way for us to be in His presence for now and for eternity. His son was His gift and because of His sacrifice, I know that my son is enjoying a life I can only imagine. A life after this life that will be so much more than my mind is capable of imagining.

Ryan's death was too soon. I will forever ask why. But I will not get an answer, except he couldn't take the pain of this life any longer. Never again will I get to wrap my arms around the son I loved so dearly. But my anguish is not for my son. It is for me, missing my son. My son is wrapped in arms far greater than my own. I can rest in the knowledge that my son is with His son and will be waiting in heaven for the arrival of all those they cherish.

Tears continue to fall as I desperately miss my Scooter, but I know there will be a day when *"He carries me in and gives me life."*

In Him,
Joyful

SATURDAY, SEPTEMBER 4, 2010

BBQ at the Barbers'

The lawn is mowed, the house is clean, and the burgers are bought. Tomorrow is the neighborhood Labor Day barbeque at the Barbers'. We are having friends and neighbors over to enjoy the beautiful weather and each other's company. Ron and I have so much to be thankful for. Our home on the park, those who let us walk through our life with them and each other. Celebrating and feeding people were two of Ryan's favorite things. Although he can no longer join us here, his enormous personality and generosity will always be a part of who we are and how we live.

Five months ago tomorrow, our lives changed. Five months later, we are learning to live with this new reality. People are so amazingly sweet and understanding. Last night, I received an incredible silver bracelet, handmade with God's love flowing into a heart. Beautiful! Receiving is difficult for me. It was breathtaking to receive this lovemade gift. Our loss has been sprinkled with a million blessings from the others that make our life rich.

Tomorrow will be a good day. We will enjoy each other and stay focused on the gift Ryan's life was to us. Good food, good friends and a day to look forward to. His brothers and sister will be here with us to lift each other up. Cheers, Ryan! The food won't be as good as if you were cooking, but we will enjoy it.

In Him,
Joyful

SUNDAY, SEPTEMBER 5, 2010

Tattoos, Songs & Poems

A tattoo is a memorial these days. So many of Ry's friends got tattoos to remember him by. Tanner's is a fly rod which symbolizes one of his brother's passions, not his. So my amazing son, Tanner, will wear a fly rod on his forearm to remember the brother he lost too soon.

Ron and I have even considered getting a tattoo. I have this idea in my head but am afraid without it drawn out that I will get to the place and

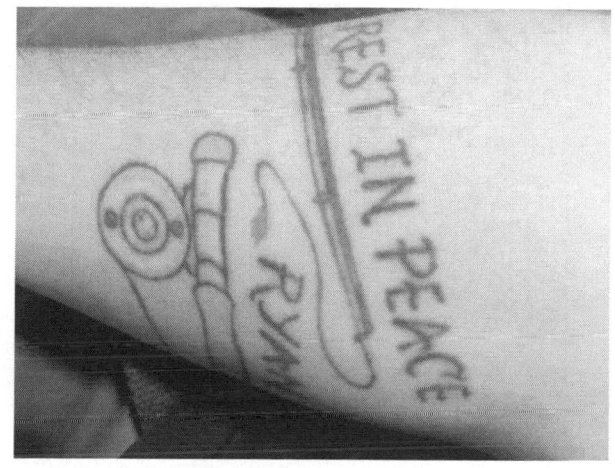

hate what they draw. Then, if I am too afraid to say anything, I will have a forever tattoo that bugs me instead of making me smile. Oh well, guess I will just wait until Tanner gets time to draw up the idea.

Ryan is remembered by so many in their own special ways. His memorial page is a gift that Brittney started and hundreds have added personal stories that explain how Ry touched their lives. From Gabe who explained how Ry was the cool kid who was kind when he was a younger geek at the skatepark, to the girl who said Ry called to encourage her every day, so she would stay on track. What a gift this will be for Lissa when she is older and asks who her daddy was. We will be able to give her a vision of her daddy from all the kind words of those who loved him.

Several of his talented friends have written incredible poems and songs that share how they loved my son. What a blessing each of these pearls from them are to Ron and me. There have been a million tears since April fifth when my son left us. There have also been a million blessings from those who shared their love of my outgoing son. He was loved. He is missed. He will never be forgotten.

In Him,   *Joyfully reflecting*

MONDAY, SEPTEMBER 6, 2010

No My Heartbreak is Not Bigger Than Yours

Being there for a friend to listen, cry and hold her hand through the rough times is more important than gifts with pretty bows or funny cards that make her laugh. I have a friend who is going through a separation. She is scared, anxious and isolating herself from all her friends and even her God. Ron and I were separated for six whole years. I didn't sleep and felt like I would never be whole again. This is the time she needs us even as she is pushing her friends away.

When she finally came to me and broke down she felt guilty. Guilty for talking about her private life and guilty because she thinks my broken heart is more important than hers. That could not be further from the truth. Everyone has things that are painful in their lives. Sure Ry's suicide makes it seem like our family trumps everyone else's issues right now. But that is not how life works. We all are here for each other when we need each other. Jenn is a perfect example of that. She had lymph nodes removed the day Ryan died to see if she needed further treatment for uterine cancer. HUGE stuff in her life. Yet there she sat five days later passing out flyers at Ryan's service for us. She didn't say, "Wait, my life is in a crisis right now, or I would be there for you." She was just there for us in spite of her own pain and fears. Same is true with Susi. She is going through life changing financial issues, but that didn't stop her from driving from another state to walk with us through Ryan's death.

Life and its tragedies are not about who has the roughest time, but rather about who is there for others in spite of their own heartaches. I pray I am always someone who can be there for others in spite of my pain. This moment finds me doing a better job of that than when I didn't have Christ walking beside me arm in arm. His love and support allows me the strength to selflessly help others even as my own tears continue to fall. Christ is not only there for us when it is a good time for Him. He is there to hold our hand even as His own heart breaks for all He sees is wrong with those He loves. If I mourn my son, He assures me that Ryan is where I want to be someday.

The song "I Can Only Imagine" keeps coming to my mind. Ryan doesn't have to imagine anymore. He is seeing Jesus face to face. So I will pray for my friend and send her little notes until she realizes she can share her brokenness with me. I can handle it, and it is harder for me to watch from a distance than to be allowed to wrap her in my arms and cry with her.

In Him,
Joyful

SATURDAY, OCTOBER 2, 2010

Prayerfully Listening is a Tough Job

As parents, we continuously walk the fine line between giving our children our seasoned opinions on life and butting in where we should not. It is difficult to convince our kids that our words and actions are always meant to protect them from life's heartbreaks.

Today, I am prayerfully considering words to guide, not control my kids' lives. My prayer is that they make choices that give them a great big world of choices in their lives. Choices that will lead them to happiness, not regret.

Young adults, my kids included, are making lifelong decisions moment by moment, some of which could impact their lives forever. Ryan's choice in April took all his future choices away in an instant. Fortunately, most of our twenty-somethings will not make a fatal error like he did. Yet, their choices on relationships, school, career and life will impact the direction of their lives.

These young adults so need our prayers as they navigate the early, independent years of their lives. Our prayer should be that they see the world at their feet and dream big dreams on the possibilities that lay before them. That they recognize that they, not their parents, hold their future in their hands and with hard work anything is possible.

My prayer for parents of young adults is to be better listeners than talkers with our now grown kids and to turn our hands up. Recognizing that God is all knowing so we don't have to be. Our job is no longer diapers or PTA. Our job is prayerfully watching their lives unfold into what God has planned for them. My heart says this is my toughest role of all.

In Him,

Joyful

MONDAY, OCTOBER 4, 2010

When I Stand in His Presence

Standing in God's presence will be amazing, and we have no way of knowing just how grand it will be or how we will react. I love the line, "Will I dance in Your presence, or in awe of You be still?" from the song "I Can Only Imagine". It is not for us to understand the magnitude of God or his everlasting presence. We are just led to believe that this will be heaven. Being with our Father in heaven will be more than we can imagine. I rest in this. My son, my father, my friend are all there experiencing His love and enjoying the essence of life everafter.

Another line that gives me peace about death is, "Jesus, lead me in." That is so comforting to me because I sure don't want to take that journey all alone. The sting of death is softened by my absolute faith that Jesus will not only have my hand but will lead me into God's presence. I don't like to be alone, especially when I am scared. Thank God I don't have to be now or at the end. For now, I will let His love flow through my heart into others so that no one I love, no one God puts in my path will have to take that journey into the unknown alone.

In Him,
Joyful

TUESDAY, OCTOBER 12, 2010

His Eyes Show His Love

My focus has been on Him so my **God-sized hole** has been filled. This weekend our family was all together except Dorothy and of course our precious son, Ryan. I am working through the sadness as best I can six months after the fact. But that fact haunts me with the truth that no more gatherings will include his smile and antics. Am I grateful for what I have? Of course! But I can't help weeping for what I have lost.

Lissa sat in the rocker where ten months ago her daddy read her stories, looking at videos of him on an iPad. Knowing he will never hold her in his arms again. It broke all our hearts as we thanked God for the pictures and videos that will remind her of his love for his little girl. I came across a card he wrote to her that says it all.

My little girl, I miss you so much. I just want you to know that even though I'm not with you right now I still love you sooooo much! I think about you all the time. I'll be going out there when I am done with probation. I am so happy you are in the care of my awesome parents. I love you and I will write to you soon! Love, Daddy

This was written when Lis was with us for seven months, and Ry was in Phoenix. How could we have known his simple message of love would be so precious to us a short time later? This card is Lissa's link to her daddy, and I will guard his words to her so she can cherish them now and when she is older.

Video images of Ry are hard to watch, yet draw me in. There is no mistaking the love his eyes convey for all of us, especially his sweet, little angel. My prayer is that she always believes what she sees in his eyes and hears in his words. He loved her even though he could not stay with us.
In Him,
Joyful

FRIDAY, OCTOBER 15, 2010

Good Spellers Need Love Too!

Don't ignore me because I can spell! Support me even when I seem strong. It just doesn't seem fair that we only support those who seem to need us. The reality is everyone needs attention and nurturing. Yes, I know that sounds harsh and ugly, but that is how I feel. I grew up craving the attention my mom gave my sister when she needed help with homework, and I didn't. In my young mind that wasn't fair. She misinterpreted it when I spelled words wrong on purpose. I wasn't showing off. I just wanted to spend time with her too. Maybe I didn't need help with homework, but I needed her time and attention just as much. It seems I am still stuck in this jealous mode when it comes to my family and still feeling left out.

I know from my own experience that I need to be taken care of even if it seems I am coping well. So just call me, hug me and tell me I can lean on you. I am not okay! My world fell apart, and I have to just live through

this nightmare of losing my precious son. So don't believe the smile on my face. Realize that I am terrified. Come hold me in your arms and comfort me. Living through this will be easier if you share my tears and help me see I don't have to make it through this on my own.

In Him,

Joyful

MONDAY, OCTOBER 18, 2010

Cheap Way Out? Really?

Cheap way out. Ryan's friend just posted that someone told her he took the cheap way out. It bothers me that someone would say that. For this person who I thought loved him to honor those words broke my heart. If anyone knew Ryan they should know that he was always about giving and encouraging those around him. He did not take the cheap or the selfish way out. His action was that of someone who never believed he deserved the love people gave him. However wrong his thinking, it was not cheap or cowardly.

This comment came on the heels of another of Ryan's friends asking if she could write a book about his life, addictions and death. I have every confidence that this book would put us through hell reliving Ryan's life. There was so much joy and so much pain in my son's short life, but I know his story as well as his death can be a lifeline to others who suffer with self doubt.

So my thought to the cheap way out comment is read the *In Loving Memory of Ryan Barber* Facebook page and see how this amazing man touched the lives of those around him encouraging everyone he met. You can bet when he lost two friends to suicide he recognized their pain and didn't cheapen their actions with ugliness. Remembering my son for the good he brought to our lives is the way most of us will continue his love even after his death.

In Him,
Joyfully defending my son

TUESDAY, OCTOBER 26, 2010

Trapped in a Crowd, Twice

Some days I just have to get through. The last two days have been "get through days" for me. Stuck in rooms full of people while the topic of losing a son and suicide came up. No escape route while the tears silently streamed down my face.

Last night at Young Life with a room full of teens and after having a blast with them, the talk was on Jesus raising a mom's son from death to return him to her arms. This was followed by a powerful song by Third Day, "Cry Out To Jesus". The video was intense, and my tears flowed as I battled to remain quiet. After all this was for each person there to absorb and not just about me. I was sitting next to a fifteen year old who could relate to the verse about children without homes. She spent two years of her life living in a car with her mom and sister. So the line about losing a loved one too soon or the one about addictions brought me to tears, but I was not the only one in the room relating personally to those lyrics. Jesus is there for each of us to meet us just where we need Him.

Today at our staff meeting after a great day with my students I was caught by surprise when the safety plan for our elementary school had a whole section on handling suicides and attempts with weapons. I sat there in the library surrounded by books and colleagues while my tears rolled once again. It felt too conspicuous to get up and walk across the room to disappear, so I just sat there trying not to feel what I was feeling.

Tonight I am emotionally spent, exhausted and numb. I can't imagine getting up in the morning and facing all my responsibilities. My calendar is jammed full for the next two weeks with so many worthwhile activities, but my heart says retreat, stay in bed, don't get trapped in another room where I can't escape or scream or throw something at the wall.

My heart is broken, but most of the time I can put on the face that says I am okay. No one can see my emotional crutches. No one thought to protect me or warn me about the content of these two talks. Why would they? Neither talk was about me. But I shouldn't have been exposed to them; shouldn't have been a part of them. I am not ready. I may not ever be ready. I will pray for strength, courage and energy to get through the tomorrows that will surely come. Until then, I will try to sleep and stay home if I must. Grief, like life, should be lived honestly. So if I honestly can't handle being out of bed tomorrow, then I will just choose to stay in bed.

In Him,
Joyful

THURSDAY, NOVEMBER 4, 2010

Waves Flow

Seven whole months.......................... Surviving in Him, joyfully mourning, tears flow, life has its pleasant moments more often now, grief comes in waves catching me off guard at times, seems like forever and yesterday. Can't we start again please?

Seven months ago............................a lifetime to go.

In Him,

Joyful

THURSDAY, NOVEMBER 11, 2010

Thanks for the Box

A box of Ryan's things arrived in the mail this week. I realize how hard it was for them to go through the stuff and pack it up for us. The stuff that he left behind will never replace having him with us. But it is important to keep his possessions so Elissa will have something to hang onto that was her daddy's.

Ironically, of all my kids, Ryan was the one that cherished my dad's stuff. He even went through a cowboy phase in high school and would wear Dad's shirts and belts. It was important to him even though he was only two when my dad died. Ry even used one of my dad's wallets. This was not only special to him, but it mattered greatly to my mom and me. It just felt like although Dad was gone for years there was still that connection.

When we lost Ron's brother, Dan, when he was twenty-five years old in a plane crash he had a bag of personal belongings on another plane. Since he was coming home for Christmas there were gifts for us among his things. I have worn the puzzle ring he sent me for the past twenty-five years. It mattered to me to remember the connection Dan and I shared, and the ring helped.

So this modest box of clothes and papers don't amount to much except that it was our Ryan's stuff. There is nothing in this box that is as treasured as the videos of him laughing and just being Ryan. Everything will be folded up and tucked away for Elissa, his most cherished daughter.

In Him,
Joyful

SATURDAY, NOVEMBER 13, 2010

Gun Case That I Certainly Don't Want

This week a person hurt me deeply, and I am not even sure if it was malicious or ignorant. My heart wants to lash out and tell her that her actions were among the cruelest I have experienced in my life. But how am I to know if her actions were hateful or misguided? My friend told me to let it go. If she did it on purpose, then she wins to see me upset, and if she didn't she won't get my heartache anyway. When the box of Ryan's things was returned this lady put the shotgun case in the box. Now this case was a cheap flimsy gun case not worth sending unless to cause pain. She knew Ryan got the gun the day before he used it from a Vietnam vet who was just being generous to my son. So she also knew that the gun case was not ours! Her point of trying to return all his things may have made this unintentional, but the nasty note that accompanied the box makes it doubtful. She is a mom. How could she have been so insensitive and unkind?

I will never know the truth, but either way it kicked me in the gut to see that among his meager possessions. My only way of letting it go is to try to believe that she is a mom too and just lashing out to protect her own daughter. My heart goes out to her for her daughter's pain my son caused by his actions. If there was one thing I could change in life it would be to protect her daughter from walking in on his suicide. No one should witness that, especially a nineteen year old. So maybe the gun case was to make us hurt just a little like her daughter is hurting. Whatever the reason her actions put a wall between us where there should have been a bridge. Our two families are connected through Ryan's death, but now the connection feels vicious rather than supportive. Her daughter lost innocence through my son's actions, but my son lost his life. Isn't our loss enough pain? Does it really lessen her pain to cause us more?

Pray for me to rid my heart of this bitterness I feel toward another mother. I don't want hate in my heart anymore than I want it in hers. Her daughter is precious to me and was before we all lost Ryan. This amazing young lady reached out to one of my Young Life girls with love and understanding long before Ryan left. We were connected because of Ryan but separate from him as well. She is also someone who reminded him of his faith and the love Jesus has for him. For so many reasons I will be forever grateful. Just wish her mom had a hint of the way I feel for her daughter instead of feeling the need to protect her by hurting us. Now I need to forgive even when I am so stunned and hurt by her actions. At this moment, I can't imagine ever forgiving her, and this is not what I want to carry with me. So please pray for God to change my heart.

In Him,
Joyful

WEDNESDAY, NOVEMBER 17, 2010

Tobacco is an Antidepressant

Dad would have been eighty years old today. The sad thing is he died at just fifty-seven from all the cigarettes, pipe tobacco and cigars that destroyed his lungs. The heartache of losing my dad was so hard. He was a fantastic, fun dad who loved kids more than anything. He never met a stranger; everyone he met became his friend. My dad was the most generous person I have ever met. If he saw that someone had a need he did whatever it took to help out. This sometimes drove my mom nuts when he would give others things that they both worked and saved to acquire.

Losing my dad to a tobacco addiction made me a firm believer that I had found the one thing that was an absolute. Tobacco was bad, absolutely. This addictive substance had no redeeming qualities, no one should ever touch it and everyone who was addicted needed to get the help they needed to get to remove it from their lives forever.

When Ryan was a teen, years after my dad died, he began smoking which simply broke my heart. Then a psychologist told me after he made a less than serious suicide attempt, that cigarettes probably saved my son's life. This man explained the antidepressant effects tobacco has and how it helps people who are depressed cope. Of course, he agreed that cigarettes were a poor choice even as an antidepressant. This was hard for me to swallow since I had determined years before that there was no upside to cigarettes.

Ryan quit smoking a few days before he took his life. Now I am not concluding that the lack of tobacco impacted his actions. I am certainly not qualified to make that determination. There were so many factors that contributed to Ryan's actions, and he had come close to this place on several other occasions in his short life. What I do believe is that tobacco is an antidepressant, and if someone is going to quit abruptly they should seek help from a professional and get a replacement antidepressant if it is recommended.

I miss my dad so much, and I still wish no one ever smoked. Smoking is a harmful act that is so hard to quit and makes people feel ashamed. The cost and the stench are not worth the benefit. There are better ways to deal with stress than lighting up a cigarette. My kids never got to know their grandpa, and trust me they missed out. He would have enriched their lives with his humor and love. We lost years that we should have had him as a part of our lives. Ryan and Dad both left us too early and left a great hole in the heart of our family.

Happy Birthday, Dad. I still miss you.

In Him,
Joyful

MONDAY, NOVEMBER 22, 2010

Downed Trees Happen

Our tree toppled over in the mighty winds last night. It was a towering poplar that came out of the ground by the roots. Since we had planned to take this tree out anyway, and it fell across the expanse of our yard barely brushing the fence, it seems like this *Act of God* was a blessing.

In life, there are times when we wake up to the unexpected. Sometimes it is a pleasant surprise, and sometimes it is a heartbreak. Eventually, we begin to understand that either way there are things in life that are not under our control. The way we get through life with its unexpected twists and turns is to follow the simple prayer. *Accept the things you cannot change and change the things you can.*

Of course, we should not sit by and wait for life to unfold. It is up to us to take life by the reins and control what we can, the best we can. But for those unexpected bumps in the road, we need to have faith we can get through them. It is not worth trying to anticipate all the possibilities in life. Life is complex and happens while we are setting our plans into motion.

In Him,
Joyful

Tuesday, November 23, 2010

Words Can't Be Taken Back

A friend innocently shared her sadness that her son would not be with them for Thanksgiving for the first time this year. Why did I lash out at her? I told her to be grateful she would be seeing him again. Ugh! I hate this. The last thing I want is for those I love to feel they have to watch their words around me. Of course she has a right to regret her son's absence on this holiday. I feel so ashamed of my harshness with this lady who is nothing but kind to me. Of course, when I called to apologize she said it wasn't necessary. It was necessary, and she was not insensitive like I made her feel. Shame on me.

This is going to be a bittersweet holiday. I am grateful to have my mom here along with my kids and grandkids. The fact that Ron and I found our way back to the love we share makes life livable. But Ryan's absence is a reminder that our family is not intact and never will be again. I am trying to see the blessings that his death brought. The fact that he won't be bugging me in the kitchen by adding weird ingredients to every dish just feels lonely. I would give anything to eat mashed potatoes complete with flax seeds and tabasco if my Scooter were just here to hug.

Thank you God, for never leaving my side. My tears flow, and I know they are proof that Ryan mattered. He continues to live in the heart of his mom who misses his hugs and his laughter.

In Him,

Joyful

WEDNESDAY, NOVEMBER 24, 2010

Thankful

Lord above, comfort me.
Give me courage, help me see.
Guide my actions, guide my words.
Let me know my prayers are heard.

God, please take this ache from my heart. Help me to cope with the pain of never being with my son on this earth again. Please let me focus on those who are here to hold and love today and tomorrow. Ron is so wise in focusing on the time we had rather than the loss we have endured. Lord, I just keep crying and can't seem to stop. I don't want to cringe when people tell me to have a Happy Thanksgiving.

There are so many things for me to be thankful for this year, but my heart feels shredded. If only I could focus on my kids, grandkids and those who love and surround me. I don't want to be so sad and weepy. God, just help me to walk with you through this season.

Amen

In Him,

Joyful

FRIDAY, NOVEMBER 26, 2010

Black Friday Angels

Mom and I had quite a Black Friday shopping adventure. Much like other years we started out at 3 a.m. Amazingly, everywhere we went we found perfect parking spots. Typically we are extremely organized, but this year we didn't even get a newspaper full of ads. So after stopping at a dozen gas stations for a paper and coming up empty handed, we just took off in the dark with no particular course of action. The only sure thing was going to Penneys for Mom's snowglobes first. As it happened we went to Penneys three times on our seven hour escapade. People we love were matched with the perfect gift at the best possible prices. We found most of the other overzealous shoppers and sales associates to be surprisingly helpful. People were patient and in great moods overall.

The highlight of our early morning was when a young guy about Ryan's age was helping me find a shirt for Tanner. (Don't worry, TMan is not good at reading his mom's blog...secret is safe.) He took us from the mannequin with the shirt halfway across the store to where the shirt was supposed to be. The size I needed was not there. So off he went to check two more places telling me to stay put! So I obediently waited hoping he was not going to get sidetracked and leave me waiting. Mom was off on her own quest at the time. He returned and told me that it was interesting that I needed that particular size. "Excuse me?" Then he smiled and pulled out the shirt I needed with a big smile on his face. I have to say, I almost hugged him. Not for finding the shirt, but for having that teasing gleam in his eyes. Ryan would have teased a customer just like this guy did. I thanked him profusely and restrained from grabbing him for a hug. I walked away with tears in my eyes and a smile on my face thinking of my son. I miss my son, but have so much to be thankful for.

In Him,

Joyful

FRIDAY, DECEMBER 3, 2010

Honestly Needing to Say No

Taking a tip from my friend the turtle and pulling my head inside my shell. It is the season to be social, celebrate life, family and faith. Though I recognize all the amazing blessings and people in my life, I am back at a place where I fear social gatherings or even a trip to my local grocers. I am praying for understanding from those who care about me as I try so hard to walk honestly through the pain of losing my precious son. Someone actually seemed confused by my tears and pointed out that this was not the first time Ry had not been home for Thanksgiving or Christmas. My mouth dropped as I realized that explaining the difference this year was pointless.

A private pity party is definitely not what I want and certainly not what I need. I am praying for guidance as I navigate this tunnel I am journeying through. So although I blogged about saying yes to life, for now I am trying to honestly and perhaps selfishly, listen to what I need to get through this season. As of today I am just exhausted as my tear ducts work overtime. *JOY: Jesus, Others, then Yourself* sometimes means taking care of yourself. Today I am taking care of me.

In Him,

Joyful

SATURDAY, DECEMBER 4, 2010

Smash Therapy

Demolition therapy today was a smashing success! I removed the tile from our bathroom shower with a hammer and chisel and made a glorious mess in the process. So the tile is all hauled out to the car and the mess is all swept into a bag. I am wonderfully exhausted. Ron has a clean surface to install the dry board and marble.

It has been a week where I just wanted to fall into bed at 4 p.m. when I got home from work every day. Spent lunchtime with the lights out in my classroom with my laptop open but with no productive work getting done. But today, I bucked up and took my hurt out on the tile that had stayed in our house too long anyway.

Tomorrow is eight months since I lost my son. The reality is that I will always miss him. But I am hoping that like a mom of a toddler that eventually stops telling her son's age in months, I will be able to make it past the fifth of the month without falling apart. Until then let me know if you have anything you need demolished. I am your gal!
In Him,
Joyful

SUNDAY, DECEMBER 5, 2010

Oh, the Pain

Kidney stones are about ten times as painful as diverticulitis. But even this pain is unbearable, just not gnaw-your-arm-off pain. When I look at the wise internet medical advice they don't necessarily correlate high stress with kidney stones and diverticulitis. At least in my body they go hand in hand. The first kidney stone I ever had was a really lousy Mother's Day when I didn't see my son, and the next was on my fiftieth birthday when one of my sons held a not so legal party while I was away.

My first bout with diverticulitis was last May when we went to Denver to get Ryan's things. Now it seems I am fighting another intestinal infection eight months later with the holidays approaching. It is clear to me that my body tenses up and protests when my emotions are high.

The good news is I already have a substitute and sub plans for tomorrow. The bad news is I am supposed to be in reading training all day tomorrow. So I took a few pills and will see if I feel better or worse in the morning. Either way, I thank God for Dr. Jimmy and his compassion and care for me and my family. I thank God for medicines too.

In Him,
Joyful

THURSDAY, DECEMBER 10, 2010

Our Christmas Letter

December 10, 2010

2010 is drawing to a close as I sit writing this letter. Each of you, who is reading this, has been an important part of our life's journey. We hope you and your family have an enjoyable Christmas season and a New Year filled with the love and support of those you cherish.

As most of you know we lost our son, Ryan, the day after Easter this year when he took his own life. Understandably, this has been the most difficult time our family has ever had to endure. People have told us our grieving process is a journey much like going through a tunnel, but there is light on the other side. Through all the tears and emptiness we have had the blessings of family and friends to help us get through each day. Ron and I are fortunate to have Cameron's family, Tanner and Natalie near so we can enjoy our children and beautiful grandkids often. Dorothy and Lis, Ryan's wife and daughter, are a few hours away, but we get to see them frequently.

*Ryan shared his faith with us last year through a song, **"What Faith Can Do"** by Kutless. This amazing song of hope and knowing Ryan's faith along with ours has been what we cling to for strength and peace. Please keep each of us in your prayers as we adjust to the loss of a father, husband, brother, son, grandson and friend that each of us loved so deeply.*

*There is a memorial page on Facebook, **"In Loving Memory of Ryan Barber"**, with incredible stories of his reaching out, encouraging and inspiring others. What a gift this will be for his daughter to see her daddy through the eyes of all the people whose lives he touched. A year ago, Ryan spent the day of Christmas baking every kind of cookie and running around his apartment building sharing with those who were alone on Christmas. His legacy is his loving and generous spirit. He will be forever missed, but never forgotten. This year, we hope each of you has others to share your day with and wish you would enjoy a few homemade cookies for Ryan and our family.*

He who refreshes others will himself be refreshed.
(Proverbs 11:25)

Merry Christmas with Love,
Ron, Barbara and family

MONDAY, DECEMBER 13, 2010

Simply Believe

Max Lucado writes the book, *John 3:16* about the simple truth of my belief. That God loves us so much that He sacrificed His only son that if we believe we will not perish but have life everlasting. What Lucado stresses in his book is that all that is asked of us is to believe. We don't have to earn it or prove we are worthy, just believe. So simple but so hard for some to do. There is just something about us humans that want to complicate things. Surely there must be more that is expected of us? Nope! Just believe, and He did it all for us: the unworthy, the hopeless, the broken, the insecure and uncertain.

JJ Heller wrote a verse in her song, "Not for what you have done, or what you will become. I'll love you for you." That is my favorite verse in the whole universe. It is not about what I have done or will do. It is about His amazing love for me. It is as simple as that. That belief is what I know and what I cling to. Ryan couldn't lose God's love by his actions anymore than I could lose His love by speeding in a school zone.

God loves each one of us, period.

I believe the reason this concept is so hard to just believe is because we don't love with that same unconditional love, agape love. People can earn our love and more tragically they can lose our love through their actions. God's love is everlasting, and His only desire is to spend time with us.

There is nothing He needs from us; it is just that He wants us. Amazing! This is my truth. This is my comfort. I rest in God's loving arms and reach for Him no matter what my circumstance. Thank God for my faith and His amazing truth.

In Him,
Joyful

THURSDAY, DECEMBER 16, 2010

Simple Heart Shaped Stone

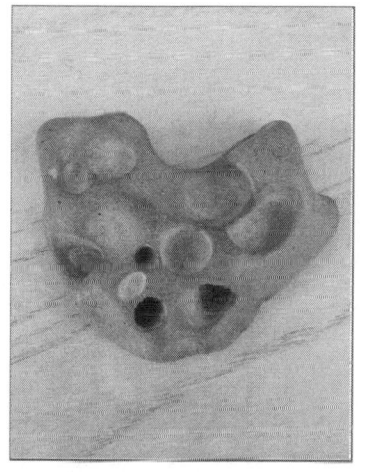 A heart shaped stone that washed up on the beach with several holes in it, yet miraculously still intact, was the gift my sweet daughter found and presented to me when she returned from Santa Barbara. Pretty ironic that it was found in Santa Barbara. This simple heart rock shares a life lesson for all of us. Though life can beat us up at times and even place permanent scars on our hearts, we are able to keep it together. Like this seemingly insignificant rock that doesn't even cover the palm of my hand, we are made to survive the tides of our lives. For decades, my children have found me a marvelous array of heart rocks. Never have I seen one so strong with such obvious battle wounds. This year this rock seems to be a perfect reflection of my own torn but functioning heart. Life has put my middle age heart through more aches and breaks than I care to list, but there is also a lasting hope present.

I know where my perseverance comes from; faith, family and friends. My heart may get pounded in the surf, but it can hold together to continue and provide hope for others. Life doesn't promise to be easy for any of us, but how we weather through is what shows who we are.

In Him,
Joyful

FRIDAY, DECEMBER 24, 2010

Missing Ryan

It is not supposed to be like this. Ron and I are getting everything ready for Christmas like life is the same. My son; oh, how I miss my son. How can I shop for Christmas Eve jammies for two sons instead of three? His bag is here with his name ready for his jammies to slip inside. Those pictures of him with Santa and the fishing ornaments are not helping me get through this safely.

Ron is back at the computer with pictures and videos just like he was almost nine months ago. A father obsessed with editing and preserving his son's precious smiles and baby laughs. How often can he sit and watch Ryan's pumpkin pie performance? Guess the number is limitless. Life goes on and then stops me cold. As I put the rolls in the oven for the dinner that he won't be eating with us someone pointed out that he was not here last year either. True, but if you knew how many times he called me you would know that we spent more time together last year than we ever had. He sent dozens of pictures of his famous cookies and wanted to know what we were doing throughout the day. Ryan didn't just call when he needed something, he called because he loved us and wanted to be a part of every moment.

His chipper greeting of, "Hello, Beautiful," never failed to bring a smile to my face. Now I know other people love me, but no one but my Scooter called me beautiful. Sometimes while the tears are falling I can barely breathe from missing him. I know this is reality, but I don't want to embrace this truth of our life without my son. If hearts can really break then we are there. Ron at the computer with that little guy's face just staring back for hours and me in bed; yes back to my bed. Our outsides are going through the motions. but the insides are crushed with the weight of our pain.

I try to look at the positives, try to cling to my faith, but my missing him is overwhelming me tonight. Never again will I judge others for not being able to handle what life throws at them. This is certainly more than I can bear. Someone wrote on a Christmas card how brave we are. What??? Brave, seriously, brave? No, we are not brave. What would brave look like? What would weak, scared and horrified look like? I don't feel brave. I am surviving, but that doesn't make me brave. I believe Ryan is in Christ's loving embrace, but I don't want him there. I want him here in my embrace! I feel selfish. I feel jealous of the man at church who told me he was so thankful to have his boys home for Christmas. I feel like throwing the decorated Christmas tree in the back yard and staying in bed.

What I will do is get up in the morning and add tears to the recipe for cinnamon rolls. What I will do is pray for strength as I smell them bubbling in the oven to golden perfection. Ry and I spent a lot of time perfecting the cinnamon rolls. This year I pray they are the best yet. I will enjoy opening thoughtful gifts from my family and watch them open theirs. This is our first Christmas with Ryan in heaven, but it won't be our last. We will cling to each other with tears flowing, thankful for the years we had with our son. Thankful for the abundant love he shared, and the example he set for each of us to reach out to others. Missing Ryan is like breathing or blinking, always a part of us even when we aren't aware.

In Him,
Joyful

SATURDAY, DECEMBER 25, 2010

Given From the Heart with Love from Heaven

For you, Dear Mother, I've given my heart...
You loved me and nourished me right from the start.
Heaven holds a special place
of wisdom, love, and Mother's grace.
To you was given not just a stone,
but a "Rock" to stand on when you feel alone.
Don't try to understand...just know I'm safe...
in the palm of Father's hand, I've received grace.
Grace to love more than I could know
Grace to heal and be free-What a deal!!
You, my mother, so calm and serene
have paved the way to the valley so green.
I'm not alone, the gang's all here.

We share, we laugh, we do not shed a tear.
So, hold out your hand...when you feel overwhelmed,
my heart lies within to bring you cheer.
I love you, Mom...
Ry

This word was given to Donna for me. What a gift.
In Him, *Joyful*

MONDAY, DECEMBER 27, 2010

A Simple Figurine

A simple figurine of a man and woman sitting with his arms surrounding her in a loving embrace was the perfect gift Ron gave me this Christmas. The love and support it represents are the best gift I could receive. Getting through the past year would have been impossible without him

here, not only beside me, but holding me up with love and understanding.

Today, I believe we will be okay. With our grandkids all running through the house and the joyful chaos that comes with a houseful of those we love. We are sitting back watching life unfold. Life is not what we plan for, but it is what we live with.

The blessing in my life is Ron by my side. This loving, supportive relationship was certainly prayed for and certainly worth waiting for. Life is not always easy, but it is worth living through. We cannot change the past, but we can look back at the joyful times we spend with those we love. Then we look forward to times that are to come with those God will bring into our lives. Today sitting on the couch embracing much like the precious figurine Ron and I are smiling for what we have and for what we lost.

In Him,

Joyful

TUESDAY, DECEMBER 28, 2010

The Perfect Gift

God lets this tender hole remain
Reminding me we'll meet again,
And one day all the pain will cease
When he restores this missing piece.
He'll turn to joy my every tear
And when I wear this necklace near

This poem was a gift from my son and daughter-in-law with a picture of Ryan and a beautiful, silver, heart shaped pendant with a hole the shape of a teardrop. What a perfect gift for this Christmas. I miss my son but cherish my children that I can still wrap my arms around. I thank God for giving me the clarity to see all the treasures I have in my life every day.

In Him,
Joyful

WEDNESDAY, DECEMBER 29, 2010

Joy to the World

My life is full of joy. That seems to be the common thread this year, and I couldn't be more pleased. My Christmas gifts will all remind me of what makes life work, Jesus, Others, then Myself...JOY. From the delicate etching on a picture frame, to three carved glass letters that were made to rest on my mantle, JOY has been added to my home and my heart given lovingly to me from family and friends. Last, but not least, my favorite Christmas song that we should sing all year: "Joy To The World...the Lord has come!"

Looking back on 2010, it has been the year with the greatest loss of my life, and yet it has brought me more love and support than any other year of my life. Of course, if I could go back and change losing Ryan, I would without hesitation. Since that is obviously not one of my options, I am hoping to reflect on what I have gained this year, in between tears and holding pictures with his goofy smile.

Christmas gathering at the Barber's - 1994

Songs have been written, poems as well. Tattoos have been created, a book is being developed, and my blog has survived in memory and in love of a son who was not here nearly as long as he was supposed to be. Friendships have become stronger through Facebook and the common loss felt by the people who loved him. It simply amazes me the outpouring for my son. Who knew the lives he was touching? Not me.

In losing Ryan this year, I gained an insight to a son I thought I knew. Oh, I knew how loving and encouraging he was to me, but I didn't know the impact he had on people he met sometimes only a few times. I wonder if he knew, truly knew, how much he improved the lives of those around him. Through this tragedy, I found out so much more about my big hearted son. My hope and belief is that he can see clearly the incredible gift of hope he left behind.

In Him,
Joyful

WEDNESDAY, JANUARY 5, 2011

Nine Months Ago

Nine months ago Ron came home late from work, and we sat on the couch watching Two and a Half Men on my laptop. My cell phone was on the kitchen counter when it rang. I did the right thing and stayed on the couch with my hubby. Then his phone rang so we thought we better get it just in case. Yeah, just in case it was an emergency. How come we, as parents, think we will be able to stop life or even death from happening when we pick up the phone? She was hysterical and just kept saying, "He is gone!" over and over and over. How could this be true? Hurt yes, dead no, No, NO!

I remember after Tanner fell eighty feet off the cliff. I always would say that my kids had a lot of injuries and close calls but no permanent damage. No life altering consequences to their mishaps. Until nine months ago when Ron and I sat on the couch with the laptop closed, clinging to each other just repeating, "No, No, NO!" How could we tell his brothers and sister? What about his grandma and Nana? We certainly weren't brave enough for the tasks ahead. Informing, planning a funeral for our son. NO! How could this be?

The sign in my kitchen that has been my life motto said, "The best way out is always through," by Robert Frost. I believe that. So we prayed and cried and planned and shared, and we made it through. Hand in hand with family, friends and our faith we are through nine months without Ryan. The first eight months I collapsed on the fifth of each and every month. Today a friend asked me how I was doing. I thought she was asking about my cold. It is not easy, but it is life, and Ryan would be glad I made it through today without falling apart. Until I began writing this post, that is.

In Him,
Joyful

THURSDAY, JANUARY 6, 2011

Two Losses That Both Matter

Two students lost a parent this week from our elementary school. One lost his dad after a valiant battle with cancer, and the other lost his mom last night. Tomorrow is the service for the dad who was loved in the community. His wife and four kids will be surrounded by family and friends. The email we got about the student who lost his mom gave no details about her death. The detail that was harshly included was that she was not an active part of her child's life. In fact, it stated that this child only saw his mom once a year, so had little contact. This fact was added for some reason. Why?

It was a reflective day for me realizing that someone at Lissa's school could have minimized the painful loss when her dad, my son, Ryan, took  his life. At the time, he lived two states away, only saw her a couple times in the last year of his life. His addictions made him realize that he needed to get healthy before he could be the daddy she deserved. Yet knowing my son and knowing my granddaughter and their love for each other, I can assure you his death was an enormous loss for this five year old. She sits and watches videos of their precious times together over and over, in the same rocker that he read her stories just a year ago.

I don't know the purpose of the explanation in the email. I hope it was not to minimize the loss. What I do know is that a third grader is missing his mom just as much or more than he would have if he had been with her every day. The love we feel is not dependent on daily involvement or even right choices. Love matters in spite of distance or mistakes.

My prayer is that every child who loses a parent or a loved one is nurtured and comforted no matter the circumstances. Whether a medical illness takes a life, or mental and emotional anguish does, the loss is still unbearable. Prayers for these families this week are appreciated.

No one should lose a child, but no child should lose a parent either.

In Him,

Joyful

FRIDAY, JANUARY 7, 2011

Wolf Weekend!

Wolf Weekend here we come! Young Life is taking thirty plus high school teens up to ski, pray and have an outrageously fun time. My thrill is that I get to be in the middle of all the enthusiastic adventure. It will be a new experience for me since I am not going as a leader this time but as a driver. So when they are in cabin time, I will be praying for them in my room instead of sitting right there. They don't even need me to help in the kitchen. God has lifted others up to fill those roles. Guess I will have time to reflect and enjoy the Wolf Lodge spending special time with my Savior. What a different experience it will be from being in the thick of the games, skits and excitement. But this year God has provided the perfect role for me: Involved with the experience and these teens that I love, but a bit sidelined. I am thankful that I am still a part of Young Life, and pray God will lead me to where my discipleship role lies in the future.

My experience has always been with Wyldlife, the middle school part of Young Life. This year that program has not even gotten started. It is devastating to realize that this is not available to our middle school friends in our little town. But God knows what He is doing, and this year would have been difficult for me to lead even WL. So I am driving high schoolers who are my heart kids from their middle school days, and I get to stay a part of their lives. What a gift!.

My heart has been so tentative since Ryan died, and this weekend I have the perfect part to play. I am welcome to be involved as much as I want, but no tasks other than driving up are required. The ride up will be awesome as everyone's enthusiasm builds for the fabulous weekend ahead. Returning home will be a wonderful, warm embrace as exhausted snowboarders share their adventures from the weekend in that worn out but comfortable sort of way.

Pray for me as I embark on the weekend and look forward to where God leads me in the future. His way, not mine is my prayer for my ministry and my life.

In Him,
Joyful

WEDNESDAY, JANUARY 12, 2011

To Comfort and Protect

1 Samuel 1:27

A mother's job is to comfort and protect her children from the moment they place our amazing infants in our arms to the day we die. Sure there are other lessons we teach them along the way, but these are the two that we are most entrusted with. We are there to wipe their tears away whether they are crying from a skinned knee from a tricycle mishap or handing them a tissue after a breakup text. Protecting them from other kiddos' cold germs with hand sanitizer or keeping an eye on them as we chaperone their first dance gives us the sense that we are up to the task.

What we hope to accomplish for our children is simple. Their lives should be safe and filled with the loving successes that we know they deserve. But moms are struck with their own inadequacies as to how effectively we can perform this on our own. Kids get cancer, bullies frighten them, drugs are experimented with, and society and reality come crashing in. Then moms have to admit that their powers, unlike their love, are limited. But that is okay. Our true power is in always being there with them no matter what life throws their way. Loving them regardless of poor choices or because of their missteps. It is the test of a mother's courage. A mom's heart is strong. It bleeds but doesn't break.

During these past nine months since my son's suicide I realize how little control I have over what happens in my kids' lives. I spent so many sleepless nights praying for my son. Now I know even in this, my prayers were answered. Ryan impacted hundreds of lives while he lived and thousands of lives since he died. Tonight I won't be worrying about my son. He is with a Father that can comfort and protect him until we are together again. The miracle is He has found ways to comfort and protect even this mother, and I know I am not walking down this path alone.
In Him,
Joyful

WEDNESDAY, JANUARY 19, 2011

Family Filled Week is my First Responsibility

Today I made a decision that feels right. At first I was afraid it was cowardly or premature, but I am now confident that it is what needs to happen. Let me tell you first off that my job and my students are extremely important to me, and I take my responsibility to them extremely seriously. So today when I saw the test schedule for state testing I knew that this is where my students' efforts are measured and decisions for each are made based on their scores. Giving them the setting for testing that allows them to shine and show how hard they have worked to master skills is so important. No pressure for testing from me. Just an opportunity to show the growth they have made and celebrate the efforts they make daily to learn.

The dates stopped my breath, even though I knew them in my head for months. Seeing April fourth, fifth and sixth on a schedule just sat me down in my chair. How will I survive that week again? Can I buck up and be here for my students, my coworkers, my responsibilities? The truth is I just don't know. I would like to be brave and show up. But the reality is my decision to not show up is more responsible. The plan for testing can be set without me so the testing won't be interrupted if I am not able to be there.

A year ago that week was the worst any family could endure. This year we need to give ourselves permission to cling to one another and not feel guilty. Besides with my birthday on the fourth and Natalie turning twenty-one on the sixth my responsibility as a mom supersedes my responsibility as an educator this year. It will be difficult walking through those days, a year since Ryan died on April 5th, 2010. I would like to spin it positively by saying Ryan wrapped his trip Home in Natalie and my birthdays.

The song "Safe In His Arms" brings tears to my eyes even as it comforts me that Ryan is safe in Christ's arms. Selfishly, I want my son here in my arms for a whole lot longer. I ache for him and the truth that on this earth I will never again hold my little boy. I hope coworkers will see that my decision to take that week off this year is me being honest about what I can and can't cope with.

In Him,

Joyful

FRIDAY, JANUARY 21, 2011

Midget Mom

Midget Mom. That is what my three boys called their little sister from the time she could speak. As soon as words began to form for this little tyke she was bossing all of us around. She just had very clear ideas of how life was supposed to be, and she was sure she was the one to keep us on the right track.

Tillie was a twenty-eight week, two pound preemie that had quite a fight on her hands from the second she was born. The neurologist told us she might be so impaired that she couldn't even suck. Scary! Just sitting beside her tiny little self was an incredible experience. It was clear even then that she was tough enough to make it through. I am aware that growing up with three older brothers was the best therapy as she always tried to keep up with Cameron, Ryan and Tanner. She never considered that she was younger, a girl or a preemie.

Here we are swiftly approaching her twenty-first birthday, and she still has what it takes to do whatever she hopes to in life. This daughter of mine was never one to let anything stop her. She was our youngest and our only girl. But she always was able to keep up with her brothers. Some would call it stubbornness. I call it determination that pushed her to become the incredible young lady that she is. Today she finds herself at a bit of a crossroads seeking God's guidance in what her next step should be. Losing one of her brothers on the day before her twentieth birthday knocked the breath out of her. Returning home from college was where she needed to learn to breathe again, and it has been so healing for us to have her here.

I know God has a path for her, and we are praying for her right direction. Her love has always been Young Life whether as a camper, leader or volunteering her time to lead the furthest out kids to Christ. It may be that God will take her to one of the far off places that she keeps finding online.

My palms are turned up, and I will accept whatever and wherever she goes next. Until then I will try to savor every day I have with this young woman who still is our Midget Mom.

In Him,
Joyful

TUESDAY, JANUARY 25, 2011

Change Me Lord

Tearful day where I questioned myself as a controlling mother, a not so great friend and perhaps even too emotional to be an effective teacher. I love my kids to a fault, but they are grown, and I shouldn't try to push them in the right direction. When will I learn that praying for them is my greatest gift, not lecturing or bullying? Being a friend means being a friend even if I need to be the one extending my hand with no hand reaching back. Lately, I have mean-spiritedly considering letting friendships just fade away. Who am I to judge why someone I love is not able to grab my hand right now? While I am in this time of drawing back myself how can I be so hard hearted? Then there are my students who deserve a teacher who is fully present every moment. Is that me? I spend my lunch hour locked in my classroom avoiding others and certainly don't spend my time productively planning. Self doubt is so consuming.

Then when I am at my lowest God sends an angel to reach out with comfort and reassurance beyond my wildest hope.

Barbara, you are a beautiful, smart, selfless, honest and creative person. You have the best advice, the purest heart and the most AMAZING family. Your children are a testament to your mothering abilities, and I can only hope to raise my children half as well as you raised yours. I love you like a second mother, and I am so happy to have you in my life. The Colsons are thinking of you and sending you love today. Why, you ask? Because like Jim Carey says in "Yes Man": Every pretty girl deserves to go to a ball. Well this is your ball, Mama, and you're the guest of honor ♥

Thank you, Freedom. I needed your too-kind and generous words today. Although I know I have a lot of changes to make in me it is helpful to hear someone has faith that I can be more than I am. Change me, Lord. Make me one who shines for you every day in every way.

In Him,
Joyful

THURSDAY, JANUARY 27, 2011

Text Locked Forever

My son, Tanner, sent me a text today that brought tears of JOY to my eyes. "I just realized.....opportunity is everywhere around me......I just have to embrace it......I love this class that I'm taking.... I truly know it's a calling for my life to help others....I'm excited about life again because I'm finally pursuing something I want to do for the rest of my life.....and I know Ryan has a big part to do with it.....that's why you two are the best parents in the world. You taught all of us to be the best people we can possibly be... and we have taken that to heart....although we struggle and fall....you two are always there to pick us back up again. I love you both very much and can't imagine not being one of the luckiest kids in the world and getting to be your son/sun :-)"

Tanner began taking an EMT class this semester. He has his massage therapist license and is going to be amazing at this new endeavor. His affirmation of his dad and me is heartfelt and the best gift any parent could ever hope to receive. God gives us pearls just when we need them most. My son is amazing, and I feel truly blessed that he is stepping out with his life and feeling direction. How proud I feel to be his mom.

In Him,
Joyful

SUNDAY, JANUARY 29, 2011

Sleepless Nights are Not Just For Mothers of Newborns

Thoughtlessness, not tragedy. That is every mother's hope in the middle of the night when they haven't received a call from their kids to know that they are alright. Last night was a long night. When a teen or adult child doesn't check in and let their parents know that they are staying out all night it unleashes the emotional demons in our minds.

We start out angry that our child didn't consider us enough to pick up the phone to call or to text a simple, "I'm okay, see you in the morning." Then our thoughts move to panic as we imagine all sorts of tragedies that could have happened to this teen or adult child we love. Quickly, we retract all the ugly thoughts of wringing their necks for making us worry as our worry ramps up. Our only hope is that they are safe somewhere, anywhere and not hurt or suffering. Later, as the sleepless night drags on we return again and again to what we will do when we finally find out they are okay. We plan to hug them tightly before smacking them upside the head and warning them to never worry us like that again.

I believe that my kids don't consciously decide when they are out with friends to ignore the frantic texts from home or to worry the bejeebers out of their parents. Just like when they were little and ran across our freshly mopped floors with mud on their little shoes; they just didn't think. Getting caught up in their own fun and adventures, they just don't even consider that we are worrying at home. They are fine and not in danger so why would we have anything to fret about? Knowing that their lack of response is not some cruel plan to disrupt our sleep doesn't help a parent in the exhaustingly, long hours of the night.

Cell phones give us a better electronic leash on our kids than our own parents had. Sometimes it is comforting to know that they can call us if they need us. But it always seems those times when we are out of our minds with real or imagined thoughts of danger, their cell phones have a dead battery or are just turned off. The reality once again is that our anger, threats and worries won't keep them safe or make them call. The mixed emotions of not knowing where our kids are cycle through until we hear from them.

Prayer helps but turning your hands up and entrusting them to God is difficult. We believe from the time they are laid in our arms as infants that our job is to keep them safe. So we call and text them with pleas to call, threats if they don't, love and prayers, and when that doesn't work we call every friend whose cell number we have trying to find them.

Then the call comes, "Mom, I told you I would be at so and so's house, don't you remember? My phone was dead. I am fine." We don't actually wring their neck, but say one last prayer of thanks that they are okay. A thought flickers across our minds, that someday they will understand when they are sitting by the phone or whatever electronic leash is available waiting to hear if their own kids are safe.
In Him,
Joyful   *Pray for me as I wait for that call.*

SUNDAY, JANUARY 30, 2011

Denver is my Battlefield

Wednesday I am going to Denver for a reading conference. Thankfully, my mom is coming with me. We will get to stay in a fancy Marriott, and I will learn a lot about eyes and brain function and how it relates to reading which I am so enthralled with. The only problem is, I will be in Denver. Only a few miles from where my son took his life. Will I be able to breathe there? Will I need to drive past his apartment? Will I even be able to function enough to go to this conference? God threw down a challenge. Not only do I need to go to this conference, but I am introducing one of the speakers, so I really can't bail on attending the sessions. No pulling the covers over my head and staying in bed where it is safe.

We will have dinner with Lisa on Thursday night and that will be hard too. I love her and want to see her so badly. But remember, she is the amazing person who went to the crematory and sat there while Ryan was cremated so he wouldn't be alone. Lisa looked at the horrific pictures of

Ryan and described them to Ron, so he wouldn't have to go see for himself what Ry looked like. What an amazingly brave lady she is. I can't think of anyone in our lives who has sacrificed more for us than she did. Losing her husband and five year old son in two separate but equally tragic accidents makes her no stranger to pain and loss. Yet there she was for us at our darkest hour. Enduring visions of horror to protect us the best way she knew how. Then she brought Ry's ashes back to us and lovingly placed them in my arms. So I must see her to hug her and thank her.

Yep, I am going to Denver and it will be hard, but I will get through. My mom will be there with me to cry together and hug each other. God will give me what I need to walk away from this conference a step closer to the other end of this tunnel. I have no doubt that I will also be able to get wonderful knowledge to bring back to my classroom. Being a teacher who can reach my students in the most productive ways will also be a take-away.

I am asking for your prayers this week as I feel I am stepping onto a battlefield of sorts, but I won't be alone.
In Him, *Joyful*

MONDAY, JANUARY 31, 2011

Let Go and Let God

Let go and let God. Such a simple command yet extremely hard to do. So often I have to physically turn my palms up to pry my will out of the way and let His will be done. The past few days have been frustrating and infuriating. My heart wants to be at peace with God in control, but my flesh wants to take actions on my own. The battle ensues. Stubbornly, I want life to be the way I want it to be with all my children protected and moving toward joyful lives.

People say God will never give you more than you can handle, but He doesn't use hard times in our lives to punish us. He uses the times that occur in our lives to draw us close. He doesn't create hardships, but He walks beside us through them. I thank God for not leaving me alone, and yet I keep trying to grab control. Why can't I learn to just let go and let God? *Trust in the LORD with all your heart, and do not lean on your own understanding. In all your ways acknowledge Him, and He will make your paths straight.* (Proverbs 3:5-6)

I have not made it through even one day living up to this verse. As I lay my head on the pillow each night I can count at least a moment or two where I selfishly tried to have my way. Trust me, I always justify myself as well intentioned. But at the end of the day,

I know that it is not up to me to guide others. Let go and let God. I still need so much work on that.

In Him,
Joyful

FRIDAY, FEBRUARY 4, 2011

Truth Equals Trust

Telling lies is never okay. Well, not telling the complete truth is not always the right way to go either. How do we explain to our kids that they need to tell the truth no matter what when we have our own little deceptions? Telling the truth, the whole truth and nothing but the truth is something that people don't do often enough. Of course, it is sometimes kind to withhold a bit of reality from others. You don't want to tell a coworker that they should not have worn that inappropriate, low cut, red dress to an important meeting or tell a friend that it really is her being unreasonable not her husband. But what about the destructive deceptions that hurt our relationships? The not telling about our purchases or keeping information about our kids from their dads.

Oh, we are good at justifying our actions. It is easy to convince ourselves that we are protecting others from the truth instead of realizing we are not trusting them with the truth. I have been guilty of this myself. Whether it was not sharing a phone call from school or letting my kids slide on a bigger crime. I remember once my friend's husband was reading the newspaper and saw his teenage son's name in the paper after being arrested. He was so hurt and angry when he realized his wife knew about it and didn't tell him.

Mothers and fathers set the example for their children. If we lie or withhold the truth from each other and other people how can we be surprised when our children are not honest with us? It breaks my heart when my kids lie to me. I want to trust them and want them to trust me with the truth. My thought has been that they should know that I will love them no matter what. There is absolutely nothing they could do to jeopardize that love. What I don't focus on is the fact that I have modeled deception for years. Not that I hid big things, but little lies are lies just the same.

One of my worst dreams since Ryan died was that I received the phone call about his suicide and decided it was too stressful to tell Ron or anyone else. A couple weeks later when Ryan hadn't called and Ron wondered why, I didn't know how I could tell him. Then I not only had to tell him Ry had died, but that I hadn't trusted him with the news. It was a terrifying dream. Of course there was never going to be a good time to share such devastating news, but everyone who loved Ryan deserved to know what happened. We dig ourselves a deep, dark hole when we lie. Rationalizing it doesn't make it okay. Hoping that the other person will never have to find out doesn't make it okay. The truth is a way of trusting those around us, and it is important to trust each other with even the hardest truths in life.

In Him,

Joyful

SATURDAY, FEBRUARY 5, 2011

Gunther Toody's, Dinner For Two

The moral of the movie *Click* was that we really don't want to fast forward life, not even the tough parts. So I am going to bravely approach the next few months and let myself (ugh) live through them however I am able.

Some of you will recognize that today is ten months. Ten months and one day since my only Easter birthday that I remember. Ten months minus one day since my incredible daughter turned twenty. Exactly ten months ago at this hour since the phone call that changed my life. My son's suicide is my reality. The love and support of amazing people is more than I could ever hope for. BUT I miss my son. Nothing else seems as good as missing him is bad.

Some things have no earthly explanation. This week I was at a reading conference in Denver where he died. My fabulous mom came with me for support. Bad weather and a hectic schedule kept us cooped up in the hotel all week. But Friday night, I decided to take us both on a drive. Our poorly planned entrance onto the freeway in downtown Denver at 5:30 made for slow going. After about half an hour of bumper to bumper gridlock we decided to take the Colorado Blvd. exit to find a place to eat. Nothing caught our eye except a restaurant called Woohoo on the other side of the boulevard. So we decided to turn around and see what kind of food they served. Mom had already vetoed Old Chicago, a pizza place.

The side street we were using to turn back on placed me directly in front of a Gunther Toody's. Ryan was supposed to start working at a Gunther Toody's on Natalie's twentieth birthday last year. Um, yes, we did decide we had to go in and eat there. Still completely unsure if this was Ry's Gunther Toody's, I asked the waitress if we were in Glendale. As expected, she confirmed that we were indeed in one of the last places Ryan had been on this side of heaven. Leaning back in the booth of this fifties burger joint, I could have seen him happily serving people here. The oldies blasting and the waitresses in their ponytails and bobby socks would have surely made him smile. This place was meant to make you tap your feet and enjoy yourself.

Out of the enormous metropolis that is Denver, God gently guided us to a place that helped me heal. Going to this conference I was unsure if I would be drawn to drive by the apartment where my son took his last breath. I had prepared myself to pray and be honest about my needs and try to follow my heart. What I didn't realize was that my Father had an even more healing path in mind for me.

Mom and I enjoyed our mound of french fries and shared some fond memories of the son and grandson that we were blessed to share our lives with. Driving home we realized we were only five short miles from the hotel. Funny how far it felt driving in the rush hour traffic. Maybe we needed to get our timing just right. If I hadn't been in the car myself I probably would find it hard to swallow how unaware we were of where we were actually headed.

The last ten months have been difficult in so many ways. The next few months as we pass his birthday and then approach Natalie's and mine with his departure day tucked right in between will be so lonely. Yet we will find blessings through our tears just as we have when we look back over the last ten months. I pray for each of us to be honest about how we are and to cling to each other for support through our loneliness.

In Him,

Joyful

SUNDAY, FEBRUARY 6, 2011

Please Take a Second to Call

My Heart,

A mother's prayers are continuous and endless. Some say no news is good news. While I believe that is mostly true, a quick call comforts and reassures me. Sleepless nights don't help my aging ticker or bring me to my knees in prayer. I am already there and have been from the first day I held you in my arms. I have stayed in constant contact with our Father who has trusted me with your care. Please just pick up the phone, call me, text me, let me rest tonight, knowing you are okay even when you are not here under my roof.

In Him,
Joyful

PS. I will let Dad know you are safe, because he is lying here beside me praying for you too.
Your Mom

MONDAY, FEBRUARY 7, 2011

Some Days

Some days I just don't want to play. Some days it feels like my life is too hard, and I just need to crawl under the covers with my fingers in my ears to keep out the pain and the reality of life. Some days I don't want anyone to comfort me or to tell me it is all going to be okay. Some days I want a daddy's lap to crawl up into to just sob my eyes out. Some days I want to scream at the top of my lungs. Some days I just want someone to punch the bad things in life right in the throat. Some days I am just overwhelmed. Some days I don't think I can take one more heartache. Some days I can't catch my breath from the sorrow.
Some days what I really need is to get on my knees and pray.
In Him,
Joyful

WEDNESDAY, FEBRUARY 9, 2011

Reassigned

A new adventure just may be what I need right now. Something to distract me with the details and the planning. So that is just what I walked into today at work. My boss brought me into his office and closed the door. Uh, oh! No, it was for a good thing. He told me he respected me and had a different path in mind for me next year. Most of you know I am an elementary special ed. teacher. So this new direction is just what I need right now. It will take me back to where I best fit in education. Already my mind is filled with ideas and planning how to fit this new role. I will be teaching a self-contained class for kids with emotional behavior needs and those on the Autism spectrum.

Just yesterday, I was in the **can't breathe** phase of grief again. Moments before this impromptu meeting I realized the parent/teacher conferences I had just coordinated with classroom teachers included meetings on Ryan's birthday. As I hurried back up the hall to reschedule these meetings, my principal caught me and asked to chat. A few potential topics popped in my head, but I didn't expect anything that would have such an impact on my life. I didn't even hesitate to accept the idea. This is God-sent. Already I am distracted from the grief I felt buried under just moments before. Yesterday, I told Ron and a friend I was sure I could not take one more thing. My bathtub was indeed overflowing, and I couldn't find the faucet to turn off the water. Then I scheduled conferences on Ryan's birthday. No, I am quite sure I cannot handle talking about reading scores on that day. Here I was worrying about getting through April with Natalie's and my birthday and Ryan's death day. Never did it occur to me that I had to make it through his birthday too. Of course somewhere in me I knew, but I hadn't mentally processed it. I can barely make it through the fifth of the month these past ten months. How will I handle this?

Just at the precise moment I needed Him, God stepped in and smoothed out my path. Yes, I appreciated my principal's confidence and kind words and this new opportunity. Mostly I am thankful for my boss's support. I shared with him the slope I felt myself sliding down emotionally and worried he would think I was unable to do my job. Instead he reassured me, told me to take care of myself first, and then in the next meeting mentioned how some of us had a lot going on yet still put our students first. Thank God for giving me this assurance that my precious students are not suffering because of my pain. I trust his words because I believe they were honest. Now I can continue to guide my kiddos without worrying that I am not what they need.

In Him,
Joyful

MONDAY, FEBRUARY 14, 2011

Underwater

Dive underwater and just swim whether in a swimming pool, clear cool lake or in the salty waves of the ocean. This is a healing escape that has comforted me through rough times throughout my life. So I don't know why I haven't turned to it these past ten months. Tonight, thank God, a friend asked me to go to a water aerobics class and it felt like I was coming home. Years ago when our first adoption ended with the birth mother changing her mind and taking our two month old from our arms, Ron and I hopped on a plane to Cancun. It was the water and sun that drew us and helped us survive those first few days without the little angel we thought would be in our lives always.

When we were finally blessed with our four children, I spent summers at the neighborhood pool enjoying the water with them all summer long. I would strap on my goggles and snorkel and swim laps with Cameron or one of the other kiddos clinging to my bathing suit straps. It always amazed me how people stared at us. What was so strange about a mom hauling her little one up and down the lap lanes with a bright pink snorkel? Okay, I will admit as much as I love water, I hate side breathing. So my snorkel allows me to enjoy swimming laps without the dreaded breathing part.

Ron and I have spent many wonderful times at lakes in the Southwest. One Mother's Day he drove me up to Lake Heron for the afternoon just to let me swim. He found one of Natalie's teen magazines and read patiently on the shore while I enjoyed the crystal clear, emerald water. That lake has to be one of my favorite places to swim. It is so peaceful!

Natalie and I came nose to nose with a friendly dolphin one summer just past the breakers on Moonlight Beach in San Diego. We were just floating on our boogie boards enjoying a mother/daughter conversation about boys when he surfaced right behind her. It literally scared me off my board! We were faster swimmers than we thought we could be getting back to shore. Later we wished we had been calm enough to enjoy the experience, but at the time it was too close for comfort or rational thought.

Each of us has activities that bring us comfort and enjoyment. If there is something that makes you feel better, more complete, try to get back involved with it. Who knows, the benefits may just help you relax and sleep better at night. I am grateful I was willing to step out and go to the pool tonight. It was so healing to be in the water.

Now I will see if it also helps me sleep peacefully through the night.
In Him,
Joyful

SATURDAY, FEBRUARY 19, 2011

April

Spring is coming! It should be a time of new life, longer days and increasing warmth. My birthday is in April, so that should bring a big smile to my heart. I am not overly excited about the month of April coming around again. April has been full of heartbreaks for me in years past.

April 1982 was when I found out for sure this body of mine would never carry a child. Endometriosis seemed to have stolen my hope of motherhood. But God had a plan for a family for Ron and me through adoption, and He saw the big picture.

April is when our first chosen son, Logan, was taken out of my arms by his birth mother after spending his first two months in my heart and in my arms. Suddenly I found my dreams of motherhood shattered. But I thank God for the time I had with Logan and continue to pray for him. Who can argue with a mother who says she has a hole in her heart? Adoption should be a win/win for all involved. Everyone must feel secure in their decision for this precious child's life. God also had our son, Cam, in mind for us, and he would have grown up in someone else's home if the plan was for Logan to be ours. Thank you, Jesus! Logan's (Austin's) mom went on to marry the pediatrician from the hospital, and he has two younger brothers. Truthfully, I couldn't make this stuff up.

Two years later, with my two forever sons in my arms we lost our daughter, Elizabeth. After an exhausting night that included a twelve hour drive, double ear infections and an earthquake, her birth mother also had a change of heart. Though we only had her for a short time she had stolen our hearts, and the grief we felt was enormous. God knew we could not have had our Tanner nine months later if Elizabeth was in our home. Once again I thank God for the children who were meant to be mine! I can't imagine life without Tanner. I received a picture of Elizabeth (Christina Marie) when she was two years old, and she was a beautiful, healthy, happy child.

Through the years, my Aprils seemed to be filled with heartache and disappointment. Then in 1990 God turned my April around with the wonderful birth of our fragile Natalie. At 28 weeks and just under two pounds she was a fighter from the first day she entered this world. My family was so afraid that she was too tiny and damaged to survive. The neurologist even said she might never even suck. But not only did she suck, she ate, grew and became stronger and more adorable everyday. April became my favorite month again. God had given me the perfect birthday present, a daughter who would get to boss around her three older brothers.

It was also April when our Tanner fell eighty feet off a cliff. He survived with a bad burn, four crushed vertebrae, and a few bruises. Ryan and Tanner threw a firecracker off the canyon near our home when they were supposed to be home studying. Natalie and I were at Cameron's baseball game, and Ron was flying out on travel. God was ever present in this situation keeping Tanner from any permanent injuries or worse. Ryan

acted as hero coming to get us to get Tanner the help he needed.

Then last year April rocked our world but not our

faith. My Ryan took his life too soon at just twenty-four years old. He had not been with us nearly long enough. The day after my birthday and the day before Natalie's 20th is now my son's death day. Or is it his trip home day? Ryan had practiced this awful thing called suicide several times over the years. He mistakenly thought he didn't deserve all the love people felt for him. Even through this most devastating time I know God sees our lives and is walking beside us. He sees the big picture and knows how our lives will be blessed with even life's most difficult tragedy.

I am terrified of April this year. Not because I expect a new heartache to present itself, but because I miss my son so desperately. The one thing I am sure of is that God will walk us through this. My faith will be strengthened even as tears pour from my eyes. God says be thankful in all things. I am thankful Ry is home and can now clearly see the life changing effect he had on so many here on earth. But it is hard to be thankful when I will never hold my son in my arms, or that Lissa will grow up without her daddy.

So I am asking all to pray for us through this spring of 2011 as we cling to each other and the faith that strengthens us. By faith, my faith will get me through to May. We will get through together.

In Him,
Joyful

MONDAY, FEBRUARY 21, 2011

A Full Birdhouse!

My amazing daughter moved out this weekend. Just across town, but it will be different with her not under our roof. She had lived a couple hours away at college, but returned home last May after losing her much loved brother. Life just got overwhelming, and she needed to be home for a bit. I thank God for that because I needed her home. Having Cameron's family, Tanner and Natalie all in our hometown has helped each of us get through the grieving process together.

One hard thing she experienced about being home in our little hometown was unexpected. Here everyone knows everyone, so people all stopped her to ask how Ron and I were coping with Ryan's death. This broke her heart! I am sure Cameron and Tanner experienced the same thing. I am sure people were not trying to be insensitive, but why didn't they ask our kids how they were coping? They lost a brother that they adored and needed support as much as we did. It somehow minimized their grief or made it seem as parents, we were suffering more. I am convinced each of them was being loving and kind and would be mortified to know how deeply this hurt. Even when we are unaware our words can cut at times.

Now you would think Ron and I would finally be empty nesters, but that may not last too long. We keep praying that his 86 year old mom will come from Arizona and live with us. That would be a blessing for all of us and keep her from being so lonely in her home. It is just hard to convince her though. Tanner is thinking of moving in for a few months while he finishes his EMT courses. It really is true about revolving bedrooms. We never seem to be just the two of us for more than a few weeks at a time. You know, we wouldn't have it any other way. When the kids were little someone bought me a plaque that said, "I prefer my little birdhouse full!" That was true then, and it is true now.

Don't think we will be lonely if no one moves in for a while. Living with a wonderful park just outside our backyard, there are beginning to be more happy sounds as families enjoy the warmer weather.

There are always scouts and Young Life to keep us entertained.

In Him,
Joyful

TUESDAY, FEBRUARY 22, 2011

Cremation Process

Tonight I felt compelled to do something so morbid I hate to admit it. Let me tell you first that next Wednesday, March 2nd should be Ryan's 25th birthday. Last night in a panic, I couldn't remember what day of the week he was born. I remembered all the other kids' days and couldn't remember his. Thank God for the internet. It allowed me to refresh my memory that he was born on a Sunday.

Today I went to my sweet Nicole's stepmom's internment. She passed away on Saturday and was cremated and interned today. Tonight, I felt driven to look up more information about the cremation process. Somehow, I just needed to know more about the final process my son went through. Horrible! As I read I found peace about the whole thing. When the kids were little I had to experience what they experienced. I put baby shampoo in my own eyes to see if it really wouldn't burn. My friend's daughter got diabetes at two years old, and her mom and I gave each other pokes and injections to see what she experienced. Obviously, Ry was not present for his cremation. He was already resting against Christ's legs and telling his stories to all who had waited to greet him and love him in heaven. But his flesh, this body that I held and hugged went through the cremation. So many times I had wiped his tears, put bandaids on his booboos and just spent time with him in my lap. That was real. His body was real. His suicide and cremation were real. Looking up cremation helped me somehow. Hopefully, it is part of the process and not me being demented.

When Ry first died Ron felt driven to view his body as messed up as it was. The policeman said even with his driver's license right there he would not have been able to ID Ryan. It was horrible. But thankfully, brave, compassionate Lisa viewed the pictures and described them to Ron, and her words satisfied him. She also stayed at the crematory while they cremated him so his body was not alone. Then she brought his ashes down to us from Denver. Lisa and Ryan shared the birthday of March 2nd. What an amazing lady and incredible friend!

Ryan and Cam fishing Colorado

We have given out so many tiny, ziplock baggies of Ryan's ashes to people who wanted a part of him. Ashes to spread in a special place or to keep for themselves. Cameron put some of his brother's ashes in a river they fished together a few weeks before Ryan died. I am so thankful for that day my two oldest sons shared. Each of us grieves how we grieve. We can't plan it. We just have to live it. One thing I have found is getting through this process with honesty is best. Even if it feels creepy to look up cremation I needed to do that. I am learning to allow myself to go with my feelings, my heart, and not second guess myself. Tonight I feel better.

In Him,
Joyful

SATURDAY, FEBRUARY 26, 2011

Happy Birthday, My Son and Dr. Seuss

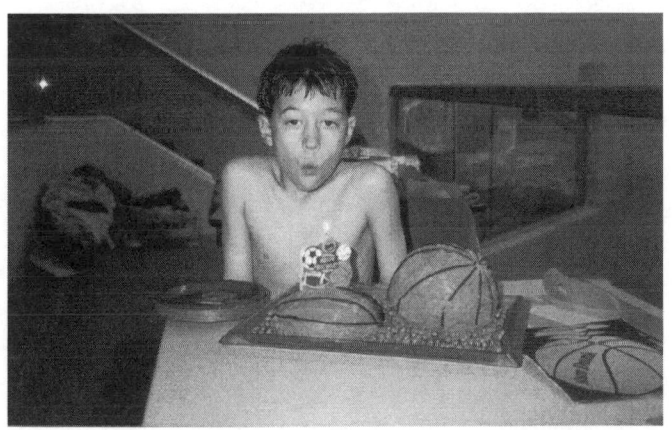

"My birfday March 2nd!" Ryan just loved his birthday. Sharing a birthday with Dr. Seuss made it even more special. Across our country kids at elementary schools dress up as his famous characters and celebrate reading. Just an extremely fun day each year. When Ry was little he was convinced that his "birfday" was more special than anyone else's because of all this hoopla.

Kids are already abuzz with which character they are going to be and how they are going to transform themselves into those unusual beings. Some will be the Cat in the Hat of course, but others will choose to be the Grinch, Yertle the Turtle, a Zook or even Sam I Am. A couple years ago Jenn and I dressed up as Thing 1 and Thing 2 for Halloween. We may need to dust off our suits for this year's March 2nd festivities. Working at an elementary school is good for the young at heart who don't want to grow up.

Kids come to school all weirdly dressed, or staff, led by Jenn, are waiting in the gym with hair spray, colorful pipe cleaners, and rubber bands to transform kids into zany characters from Seuss' much loved stories. This is a day of fun and learning when we can combine a love for reading with creative chaos. The Mrs. Souza led student council members will have a few fun tricks up their sleeves to make the day even more exciting.

I am so glad my son shares a day where it is impossible to dwell on sadness with all the joy and life filling my school and my day. I am blessed to be in a job I love surrounded by children and staff I adore. No one knows how much their smiles and hugs really mean to me because my words are not enough to express the comfort they give.

I will retreat to my room when I need to this year and enjoy the overflowing happiness the rest of the day. Ryan should be twenty-five on March 2nd this year. The twenty-four "birfdays" he had were always filled with friends and fun. Happy birthday, Scooter, and happy birthday, Dr. Seuss!

In Him,

Joyful

MONDAY, FEBRUARY 28, 2011

Somebody Loves You

I first became obsessed with this song when we lost our first son, Logan, when his mom changed her mind about the adoption. We had loved him and cared for him for two months and didn't know how we were ever going to get through losing him. Now we are wading through the grief of losing our Ryan. His twenty-fifth birthday should have been this Wednesday, March 2nd. Ron and I find ourselves swallowed up with missing him. This song just seems to soothe my heart. I do know he is okay, but we are not okay without him.

We love you, Scooter!

"Somebody Loves You"

by Crystal Gayle

In Him,

Joyful

TUESDAY, MARCH 1, 2011

Breathe In, Breathe Out

Breathe in, breathe out, breathe in, breathe out. I just need to breathe. Today everything made me cry. A mom was bringing cupcakes to school when I was doing crosswalk duty. Breathe in, breathe out. No more cupcakes for Scooter, and he won't ever be there to take them to school for Lissa. I can't breathe with the weight of this pain. I pray we can get through the next day without our son. Tonight Natalie just sat on my lap, wrapped in my arms sobbing from the loss of her brother. How do we breathe our way through this? This is definitely what being overwhelmed with grief feels like.

God, just walk beside us, hold us close as we seek to maneuver through Ry's birthday. How can it be this hard? It is harder than I expected, and the day isn't even here yet. Thank you, Lord, that my kids are all going to be together tomorrow. Everyone except Ry, who should be the birthday boy. Please bring us peace and acceptance of this unchangeable truth that we must live with. Amen

In Him,   *Joyful*

WEDNESDAY, MARCH 2, 2011

He's My Son

What he needs right now is you, Lord. It is hard to let go of my son, but I have to rejoice in his new reality. He is wrapped in Christ's arms, and that is the hope I had for him all along. Thank you Lord for taking him Home. The song, "He's My Son" by Mark Schulz, was one I listened to and prayed so often when Ry was struggling through life. Listening to it

now I know that this heartbreak I feel is my loneliness for him. These feelings are so valid, but so is the fact that the words I prayed in that song over and over have been granted.

So you see my son has all that he needs in heaven. The peace and grace he couldn't let himself accept here on this earth. Though Ry didn't get the chance to grow old, I am trying hard to figure out how to live here without him. I am comforted that he is no longer tired, scared, or feeling the weight of his mistakes. God has enfolded him in His arms and assured him that he is valued and loved by all whose lives he touched. I am sure he was shocked to hear God's highest praise for the life he led. Where he saw failures others saw loving acceptance.

His acceptance and encouragement for everyone mattered so much more than the mistakes he made. It is clear that all those nights we prayed God did hear and knew better than we did the path to Ryan's eternal life.

In Him,
Joyful
Happy Birthday, Scooter!

THURSDAY, MARCH 3, 2011

Scooter

How Scooter Got His Name

About a year ago I found one of Ryan's baby shirts and hung it in my closet door to show him when he got home for the holidays. When we adopted our kids we had a tradition of selecting several names and then name them when we held them in our arms. We were in California the day Ryan was born in Arizona, and the hospital called and required a name to put on his birth certificate. I tried to tell them we just could not name a child without first seeing and holding him. They didn't care. So we gave him the name Scooter from the outfit Gramma Pat bought him. We were able to hold him for the first time on day three, and quickly gave the lawyer our camera, who took our picture. We then unwrapped our son for the first time so we could marvel at him and touch him from head to toe. We then settled on the name RYAN, which means Little King or Noble One. The shirt still hangs in the same place in my closet. Our Ryan continued to have the nickname Scooter the rest of his life.

In Him,
Joyful

FRIDAY, MARCH 11, 2011

King of Hearts

Jenn is right when she says we judge others' outsides by our insides because I am keeping up a pretty good facade for the world around me. But my grief from losing my twenty-four year old son to suicide has cycled back to where it is hard to keep food in my stomach or to even sleep at night. Drinks of any kind have been tough on my stomach through most of this journey. Don't get me wrong, I could use the food repulsion to lose weight and that would be a blessing. In fact, my friends and I have been jealous of those who just aren't interested in eating in the past. But I am finding it hard to even function in my daily routines right now. Tears flow, and I yearn for my bed with the door closed tight.

So tonight I had a breakthrough! Ryan can be represented by the multitude of things in his life he treasured like his friends, cooking, fishing, skateboarding, shot glasses (unfortunately) and the list goes on. But here I sit at 2:20 a.m. and it hits me.

THE KING OF HEARTS is a perfect symbol for Ryan! His name means king and he has left his incredible loving spirit in the corner of all our hearts. Perfect! This makes me smile so much just thinking of it. From now on when any of us plays cards we can give a quick kiss on the king of hearts for Ryan and take the opportunity to send up a quick prayer for Elissa and Dorothy. I simply love that! Miss you my son, the King of Hearts. His sweet friend, Nicole, even got a crown tattoo on the back of her neck for my sweet son.

In Him,
Joyful

SUNDAY, MARCH 13, 2011

Helpless

My friends are here for me by simply being my friends. I got a call yesterday and spent time today with two of my lifetime friends. They both expressed concern over not knowing how to help me get through this rough season. I know how helpless they feel because I feel helpless in trying to support Ron and the kids through this. But what I wish I could convey to them is that the mere fact that they are in my life is a comfort and support. Guess I need to remember this myself.

I know how helpless friends feel as they watch Ron and I grieving for our sweet son. But I pray they can take comfort in knowing God gave them to us as a gift to get us through even this. Their love and prayers matter even when it feels like there is nothing else they can do. I pray for comfort for all those we love and peace for all of us. It will be May eventually, but first we must weather this.

Thankfully, we are not alone!

In Him,
Joyful

SATURDAY, MARCH 19, 2011

Borrowed Courage

My daughter's courage amazes me. Last summer, just a couple months after losing her brother she stepped up to let her pain and God's love touch others. She volunteered at a Young Life camp for a month. The summer staff of college students and high school work crew were there to serve for Him these middle school campers. Some of these kids had never heard of Christ, others felt they were way too cool for Christ, and still others were afraid to trust and accept His unconditional love.

How powerful was the image of these young adults not only accepting His love but being willing to take time out of their busy lives to serve for an entire month. The example they set was most powerful. These leaders bravely stepped forward with **Cardboard Testimonies** to share heartaches Christ had walked them through. Each simple piece of cardboard held a personal hurt on one side and a way God blessed them on the other. My brave Natalie put the pain of her brother's suicide on that piece of cardboard and how God had walked beside her on the other.

Her grief was raw, and it blows me away that she loved those kids enough to selflessly put her pain out there. Letting them glimpse into her broken heart and see that her strength came from the One who never left her side was such a gift. Her hope was that Christ could become a real part of each of these youngsters' lives so they didn't have to walk alone through life's hardest moments. I was enormously proud of her last summer. Only God knows how many hearts were moved toward Him because of her willingness to be vulnerable and real.

Tomorrow, I am doing a **Cardboard Testimony** in church. Tears fell as  I practiced today. I am not confident that I have the courage it will take to walk up there and share with others that my son took his life. But I pray I can be as strong as my daughter and let others see how God has walked with me through this storm. Emmy has agreed to be there to support me and others will be praying. Natalie has set the example, and God knows I can do this with Him at my side. My

card said: **My Son's Suicide/ Faith, Family & Friends**

In Him,

Joyful

TUESDAY, MARCH 29, 2011

Chatting With Ry

I find myself recalling the conversations I had with Ryan a year ago as we approach the one year anniversary of his death. The last few weeks of his life he called me every day for encouragement on his new health plan that he and Arianne were doing. They were working out twice a day and eating healthy. Each day he would call and say day three or day seven and let me know how great he felt while not drinking and getting in shape.

A couple weeks earlier he had run into Moss and Colter from his high school days. Back then Ry was the skinny, fit guy, and they both ragged on him for his beer gut. He took this as a challenge and began his fitness phase. I loved it because he called to check in every day. I am grateful for all the pictures Arianne took of him the last weeks before he died. He was more willing to be photographed because he was feeling good about himself. A few days before he died he even gave up his cigarettes.

We spent April Fool's Day chatting several times as he tried to come up with the perfect prank for his dad. He wanted so much to catch his dad off guard. I loved those talks as we conspired for just the right "gotcha" that Ron would believe. We never did come up with one, but those calls scheming will forever make me smile.

Since my birthday was on Easter, I spoke with Ry several times that day too. He was always so concerned that we knew how much he loved us, and how important we were to him. That day he was sad to not be with

Elissa hiding and hunting Easter eggs and regretting not being with us for Natalie's and my birthday breakfast. No way would we have been going out to eat if Ry was here. He would have insisted on cooking to spoil us. Of course he shared all his dreams for the new job at Gunther Toody's and just knew he would be running the place before long. Ry always dreamed big. But with his personality he could have charmed anyone into letting him do anything.

I am enjoying my memories, but oh, how I miss my son.

In Him,
Joyful

WEDNESDAY, MARCH 30, 2011

His Voice

An old phone full of photos is the treasure we stumbled upon today. Texts from Ryan telling us he is living the good life and loves his job. Amazing when we lose someone how every picture and every word becomes a pearl that we hold tightly. When Ron's brother died twenty-five years ago we didn't have his laugh or his voice recorded. That was so sad. He was only twenty-five years old, and we lost his amazing laugh. I am so thankful for all the videos we have of Ryan to cherish and to share with his sweet six year old, Lissa.

When she is here she sits in the rocker and just watches video after video of her daddy on Ron's iPad. Tears stream down her soft, little cheeks as she remembers how much he loved her and how he left way too early. It is going to be a challenge to help her understand that his suicide in no way changes the incredible love he had for her. Suicide is not always a choice. I know how judgemental I was of anyone who ended their life before my Ryan lost his life to this horrible act. Having talked to him for hours that day, I know that this was the furthest thing from his mind. He had plans, and he was looking past that terrible evening. Ryan was not at a place where he chose suicide. It seems to me now that suicide chose him. This is so hard to express, but I know my son, and he would not have chosen to leave us. Even though his death was at his own hand it was not his choice. The circumstances just lined up and in a blink of an eye, a squeeze of a trigger, it was done. No do overs, no taking it back. He was gone.

My only comfort is that Christ was right there to lift him into His arms the moment it occurred. We were even blessed by the circumstances to be together to cling to each other. Natalie was whisked into the van with Cameron and Brittney. Tanner was home within minutes. Dorothy and Elissa caught the train at 5 a.m. to be here with us. That night we spent the wee hours of the morning and into the next day just holding onto each other. God held Ryan, and we held each other and prayed as we somehow found the strength to tell his grandmas and the rest of those who loved him of this tragedy. We prayed for the strength to get through this new reality. Putting together the service and details that cannot be put off were done with prayer and the loving support of those who just came to take care of us.

This next week is going to be rough, but we will be together in our sorrow and loneliness. Remembering the awesome times we shared with Ryan, and the fact that he is where he will never doubt his worth ever again helps us through.

In Him,

Joyful

MONDAY, APRIL 4, 2011

Peaceful Birthday

A blanket of peace comforts me. On my birthday I am loving being with my sweet daughter and amazing husband at the beach in Santa Barbara. Breakfast in bed with double doors open to a veranda and the ocean help create the mood of peace. To think a year ago I was up at dawn for Easter Sunday service, next breakfast with Natalie, and then the afternoon being there for Jenn as she got ready for a second surgery for cancer. The following day our world changed with Ryan's unfortunate death. The incredible emotions of the last year have indeed brought me to my knees more than any other time of my life. New relationships and the pouring out of love from forever friends as well as those who are new in my life because of Ryan give me strength. Tears have flowed as we cling to each other honestly missing our son. I thank God that Ron and I have been a strength to each other even when it was hard to take a breath in our overwhelming grief.

I have dreaded this week for months. A year after losing my precious son I imagined it would be one where I just wanted to crawl under the bed and scream into my pillow. My understanding boss gave me the whole week off to just be here with my family for Tillie's 21st birthday and this first anniversary of the day that crushed our hearts. Yet now that the time has come, I feel such peace. For a moment I felt pangs of guilt for not being more devastated or sad. Then it occurred to me that this peace is God's gift delivered through the prayers of all of you. Your prayers, love and support are like a warm blanket keeping me calm through this week. Tomorrow there may be tears or maybe not. Whatever comes I will embrace. Living honestly with my feelings has been a real part of the past year and is one more blessing I have received.

So today as I become eligible for senior discounts and in a couple of days when Natalie becomes old enough to have a glass of wine at a restaurant, we will enjoy the beach and lazy vacation days. Remembering Ryan and sprinkling a few of his ashes into the salty surf will certainly be a part of this trip. Cam and Tanner are both taking the day off tomorrow to spend it together; brothers spending time together reliving the good times they share. My prayers are with them, and I thank God for them choosing to turn to each other for strength.

This is our family story which now includes Ryan's death, and one thing I am convinced of is this: If I had a window to the future and could have seen what my life would include, from infertility to adoption, from vows to separations, from cliff falls to suicide, my choice would have been to live my life this way again. Not that I don't have regrets; of course I do. But I feel fortunate for all the times I have had with my Ron and our kids. I thank God for the years I had with Ryan and praise Him for the gift of Elissa and Dorothy. Each and every heartache has brought me to this place in life where I am firm in my faith and relationship with my amazing Savior and am living my life with those I love. Rest in Christ's arms my son, and know I love you now and always will.

In Him,
Joyful

TUESDAY, APRIL 5, 2011

Twenty-Four Years and a Lifetime of Memories

One year, 365 days, 8760 hours without my son. No wait; 24 years, 8794 days, 211,056 hours of life with my son. This is a day to celebrate not his death, but his outstanding life. Ryan was a gift to all of us, and though he is not walking the earth any longer, his love and encouragement continues to be a force in our lives. Ryan was a unique person who could and would make anyone feel like they were his most favorite of all. Ron and I have heard so many say that Ry was their best friend. How can that be? Most people only have one best friend. But you know each of them is right. Ryan had more best friends than most of us have casual friends. There was just something about that guy that made people feel accepted and valued. If only we could bottle his personality to dispense to others the world would be a more accepting place.

This is a day that I celebrate the life of my son and grieve that I no longer get to pick up the phone and hear him call me beautiful. I was beautiful to Ryan; we all were. He saw past the physical and emotional scars to the person that was worth knowing. Bringing out the best in others was as simple as breathing for this man. Now I know Ry was not perfect, in fact far from it. He never believed in himself as much as he believed in those around him. I only pray that now that he is home in heaven he is clear about the impact his words and love had on those around him. Ryan

tended to look at his mistakes rather than his accomplishments. That is so sad to me. JJ Heller wrote, *"not for what i have done, or what i will become, who'll love me for me?"* Ryan loved others and was tolerant of people's oddities. What a treasure to have that outlook in life. Not to always be jealous or condemning of others but to encourage and sing others' praises is the way we should all live.

We are spending today at the beach reflecting on the happy times spent as a family with our son. Bet I will find a perfect heart rock and know he would have picked it up and handed it to me with a smile if only he still could.

In Him,
Joyful

SATURDAY, APRIL 9, 2011

Time For Reflecting on Our Trip

Returning home always feels so satisfying even when I am on a most wonderful vacation. This was the first time I have ever taken the train across the country. I totally recommend it. The families on the train were having fun together playing cards and snapping photos as beautiful scenery flowed past the windows. Everyone seemed friendly and willing to share their life stories or just let you read if you preferred. I am positive this will not be my last train trip. Heck, letting someone else drive was amazing! This much needed trip was exactly what the three of us needed. The prayers you all sent just made our trip a perfect, peaceful retreat. Now I feel confident to be able to get on with life on the other side of the first anniversary of losing our Ryan. We enjoyed going through the videos and pictures on the trip as well as spreading some of his ashes in the Pacific. What a wonderful way to spend our birthdays. In Him,

Joyful

Ron wrote a sweet tribute that I would like to share:

IN THIS BOX

IN THIS BOX are the tangible remains of one we love and now miss so much. On the evening after Ryan's memorial service we had a ceremony and committed his ashes into the bonfire. Over the next week, family and friends from all around cleaned out every last bit of ashes and began their journeys of remembering and dispersing his ashes to their special places. His ashes have been taken back to Alaska, the east coast, the northwest Cascades, any number of favorite fishing spots in Colorado and New Mexico, Oak Creek Canyon, favorite beaches and surfing areas, the snow corniced ridges of the Sangre De Cristo mountains, the fabled San Juan River and who knows where else. I've carried his ashes with

me in this little box for the last year as I have traipsed around the west chasing shadows at ancient calendar sites. The hand on the box symbolizes a common glyph we find, where a thousand

years ago someone else left a tangible sign of their presence here on earth. This week we journey by train to the coast to rest, remember and return his ashes to the beloved beaches. As the last rays of sun are setting I sprinkle his ashes into the water. It's only fitting that in the background a school of fish is breaking the surface, and we know what Ryan would be doing right now if he were here.
Luv ya miss ya,
All of us

TUESDAY, APRIL 19, 2011

A Special Love Between Daddies and Their Little Girls

One of my amazing high school friends posted this on my Facebook. *Her daddy may have taken his own life, but he never meant to leave her. Suicide happens; people don't choose it.*
It made me cry. I have to believe that though my sweet granddaughter lost her daddy when she was only five years old, we will be able to remind her of all the special times they shared and how much he loved her. She sits in the chair watching videos of the two of them with tears rolling softly down her cheeks.
In Him,
Joyful

MONDAY, APRIL 25, 2011

More Than One Soul Dies in a Suicide

My amazing daughter, Natalie, turned twenty the day after her brother took his life a year ago. This year, at twenty-one, she continues to amaze me with her heart. She has started a creative 365 project with her newly discovered love of photography. Most of us approach life by sticking our toe in the water when we try something new. Natalie blows me away because whatever she attempts she just dives into the deep end and feels

secure she will be able to swim.

Her photo essay on grieving the loss of a brother is powerful and moves me to tears. I could not be more sorry that she has had to endure this pain or more proud of how she is maturing through it. This daughter of mine has an intense faith and stands firm in her beliefs. Not only does she know God, but she actively works to make Him known.

I have had the honor through the years to serve beside her in Young Life as she allows Christ to use her to lead young teens to Him.

In Him,
Joyful

More Than One Soul Dies In A Suicide

A year ago this month, my brother Ryan took his life. This is what's on the inside that rests until provoked. My pops used to say, if it can't be fixed with duct tape, it can't be fixed at all. So what about this one?

SATURDAY, APRIL 30, 2011

Texas Road Trip

Sometimes a road trip is just what a relationship needs to bring it back to health. Tillie and I took off Friday at noon for Austin, Texas which according to Google Maps will take about thirteen hours each way. We are going to get her things, see the sights and make it back home by Sunday sundown. Deep breath! So here we are on Saturday afternoon. She is packing, and I am catching up with internet play. The trip here was amazing, and as my daughter shared her incredible taste in music with me, we laughed, reminisced and dreamed about the future. She is so excited since she just got a job on a school bus with special needs students. Her zest for life makes me smile. I am watching my sweet girl unfold her wings with a confidence that was missing a few weeks ago. The change started on our train trip to Santa Barbara. Ron and I both noticed little changes that told us God was working on her heart and reawakening her to the plans that are possible in her life.

Our son's suicide knocked all of us off our feet, but his close relationship with Tillie coupled with her assault the year before really took her hopes away. She has continued to stay connected with her faith but interacting with friends and moving on in life seemed beyond her at times. Oh, how

we have all prayed for her to come back to realize what a treasure she is. Knowing that she had guilt about her brother crushed me. Even as his mom I know he knew we loved him and that logically that love should have saved him. But his path was no one's fault, not even his. Mental illness and addictions are more powerful even than a father's love for his little girl. Natalie misses Ry just like we all do, and it was a blessing on this trip to share the joy we had with him rather than dwell on the tragedy of losing him.

This weekend is a gift; a gift of time with my daughter who seems to be opening her eyes from the pain and looking excitedly toward her future.

Who knows? In a year or two we may be taking a music filled trip to Santa Barbara to get her settled in school there. God knows.

In Him,
Joyful

SUNDAY, MAY 8, 2011

Highs and Lows Today

This emotional Mother's Day has tuckered me out. We started at church with them expressing the numerous tasks of a mother and the enormity of her heart. I was overwhelmed with missing not only my precious Ryan, but Logan as well. There have been few moments when I have felt my inadequacies contributed to Ryan's death. God has protected me from guilt through most of this grieving process. But today when the pastor was talking about nurturing and guiding I just lost it. The tears flowed and the day's festivities seemed to loom in front of me like a mountain that is too high to climb. I left and went to the car and called Susi. She let me flush my uncertainties while she reassured me that Ry knew just how much he was loved and didn't leave because I made mistakes. Comforting!

Then it was off to church #2 where the service was on the beauty of women regardless of their outsides and in spite of the mistakes they have made. Perfect, I was so glad I had not opted for crawling under my bed after all. We then had a herd for lunch, time relaxing with my new book in the sunshine, and later Emmy made dinner for all of us.

God has a plan even when I don't feel safe or strong enough to take another step. When I put one foot in front of the other I am rewarded with powerful healing emotions. Today was a perfect example of that.

In Him,
Joyful

WEDNESDAY, JUNE 15, 2011

Heartfelt Song

Justin wrote this incredible song for Ry. Incredible talent, amazing

RYAN BARBER.... MY BROTHER

There's a part of me that wants to leave this world behind
It's a side of me that's been broken many times
In our darkest days still tryin' to find the light
Though hope lingers, true happiness is hard to find
I've got no strength in these arms to fight anymore, no
I've got no will in these legs to help me carry on
My wings are broken and my faith is lost
Can't find the heart to carry the price this life has cost
Cuz I'm fallin', yea i'm fallin'
I'm fallin', oh...
I've been hidin' in the darkness for far too long
Still tryin' to chase the moments that have come and gone

I've been sittin' watchin' life pass from the shoreline
I wonder what might happen if i left it all behind
Could i forget the life i led?
Would i ever cross your mind.
The angel on the stairs, calls me to her
Dancing on silver clouds, on a full moon rise
Carry me to that place we're bound to find
I'll come to you in dreams seeping thru the blinds
Remember how I touched you, remember how i once was
I'll be here waitin' for you, I can't wait, no
I can't wait to see you again.
Justin Nunz

FRIDAY, JUNE 17, 2011

Time Enough

"One more hour, just one more day," is what people say they would trade anything for. When we lose a loved one we just desperately yearn for a bit more time with them. I know I would love to just take Ryan's face in my hands and gaze into his eyes or sit and listen to one more whacky story my dad used to tell. But if I seriously had the chance to bargain for that time, I would choose to pass.

If the deal was that I could have more time in exchange for losing them all over again I would pass. The reality is that the grieving process does include time to heal our hearts. Losing a loved one is unbearable, but with time we heal. Not that we don't always miss them, but the pain eases and life returns to a new sort of normal.

If I had an hour with them what could I say? It is not for me in this life to have the answers or wisdom that they have acquired in heaven. We are on different paths that will come together again but not in this world. So for now, I will remember those I have lost with love and smile at the greatness of their personalities. But I will be satisfied that the time I had with them was enough until we meet again.

In Him,

Joyful

THURSDAY, JULY 21, 2011

Comfort Others as You Are Comforted

It was so difficult to watch another family grieve the loss of their precious twenty-one year old Nicky. I pray for peace over them as they grasp how permanent this loss is. More than once today I heard someone say it has to be a mistake, a joke, a misunderstanding. He can't be gone. Natalie and I had the exact same conversation about Ryan when he died. The love we have for the ones we love is so much a part of us. It is difficult to believe we can move forward in life with a loss so great. I heard someone speaking out of a need to comfort saying everything will be okay. Though I held my tongue, I wanted to dispute that. It will never be okay to go on without Ryan or Nicky, but we will. The pain will ease, but life will forever be different than before they left this place.

Pray peace for the Naranjo family. I pray we can be a comfort for the loss we share. It is not a group we chose, but the group of parents who grieve this loss is growing too rapidly in our town. The least we can do is be there for each other.

Christ, the Father of compassion and the God of all comfort, who comforts us in all our troubles, so that we can comfort those in any trouble with the comfort that we ourselves received from God. For just as the sufferings of Christ flow over into our lives, so also through Christ our comfort overflows. (2 Corinthians 1:4-5)

In Him,

Joyful

FRIDAY, JULY 29, 2011

Lissa's Words

Love Daddy, from Elissa

I remember ice skating with my dad. He teached me how to skate and I always falled down on my little hiney. We took pictures. We had hot cocoa and we didn't even spill. He showed off skating backward and turning circles around me. It was awesome fun!

When my Daddy and Uncle Tanner were little boys they wore clown suits and cowboy boots. Noni still has the clown suits in the toy box. I put the clown suit on once and I felt hugged like when I wear my Daddy's fishing jacket. I am sad because I miss Daddy a lot. I miss him the most all the time.   *Lissa*

THURSDAY, OCTOBER 13, 2011

Grieve Honestly

"'I wouldn't have chosen it, but since it did happen, I chose how I was going to respond to it.'" Keeping God close is my comfort and strength.

Oh, how I miss his ornery laugh. Grief comes in waves. Talked to a couple of close friends about your loss. I still have days when I need to crawl under the bed, days I can laugh about wonderful times together, and days I just need to punch something. Faith, family and friends get us through each storm in life. But being honest about how we are and what we need is extremely important. In most situations in life we try to just buck up and push through, but with grief it is so important to honestly allow yourself the healing.

In Him,
Joyful

SATURDAY, NOVEMBER 5, 2011

Just Turn Around

Plans don't always pan out. Some days you just have to turn the car around and drive in a different direction. That is how my week has been. On Tuesday, Tillie and I drove forty-five minutes to sign language class. We arrived early and sat in the parking lot. Within minutes we both agreed we were exhausted and wouldn't be able to focus. As I was driving home listening to my brilliant daughter, I knew I didn't regret making the seemingly wasted trip to Santa Fe.

Last night, I was looking forward to going to see Kutlass live, on the fifth no less. Kutlass sings "What Faith Can Do" which had a great impact on our Ryan's life and on us through his death. Since he left us on the fifth I thought it was perfect to see this amazing group of young men perform a song that so impacted my son and those I love.

On the way down, my friend Pat called and told me her sweet granddaughter had fallen. I was one hundred miles from my house, but I knew I was not up to going to this sure-to-be-amazing concert alone. Tillie and a friend were going to meet us later when they got off work, but the thought of going alone to save seats was more than I could manage. Although I didn't want to flake on Natalie, I knew it was time to once again turn my car around and head home. Wasted trip? Not really.

Tanner is home for the weekend, so we ended up watching Whitney, a hysterical new sitcom, together and laughing our heads off. I am so blessed to have my children in my life. With each passing day I miss Ryan, but his life and death taught us to cherish moments together.

Yesterday it has been nineteen months since my son took his life. I have been obsessively playing "I Can Only Imagine" over and over. Knowing Ry no longer has to imagine but is seeing Jesus face to face comforts me. But oh, how I miss his silly laugh and goofy smile. I thank God for taking better care of my son than I ever could. When will I learn to stop worrying about those I love and simply pray?

In Him,
Joyful

THURSDAY, NOVEMBER 18, 2011

Missing Daddies

Daddy's birthday yesterday was difficult and made for a tearful day for the first time in years. Today I am going to the funeral of one of my Young Life girl's father. She is a junior in high school and loved her dad. He was one of those involved dads that we always saw in the halls at school, volunteering for projects and driving kids to and from activities. Life got the better of him last week, and he ended it all. So hard to understand that act. There is just no way to understand it because it is not a rational decision.

Again I am reminded of how judgemental I was before Ryan made that same choice. He was such an empathetic person always thinking of others' feelings and reaching out to comfort and encourage. No way did he think through the consequences of his last act, or he would never have ended it that way. My feelings changed about suicide. It is not selfish. It is irrational and desperate, but not selfish.

So today I will somehow make it through this service for my girl's sake. She was one of the amazing teens who were there for me after I lost Ryan, and I will be there to love on her during her rough months ahead. Putting others before myself even when it is hard is what Christ would do. So I will lean on Him and hope she can lean on Him as well. Today is not about me, but boy, do I miss my dad and my son. My eyes keep weeping at the thought of her young heart losing her daddy in such a tragic way.

In Him,
Joyful

SATURDAY, NOVEMBER 26, 2011

Family Filled Thanksgiving; No Time to Write

My life has been filled with four generations of wonderful family time. Here it is Saturday, and I haven't blogged since Tuesday. That is great news! Writing matters but can wait as I spend time laughing, sipping tea, chatting, watching the grandkiddos play at Noni's park and eating together.

Ron and I took a moment in the kitchen for a quick, tearful hug to miss our Ryan but having our other three amazing children and their families and friends here made it a joyous Thanksgiving weekend. Black Friday fun was a success as Mom and I have all our gifts purchased at a fraction of the price and each is carefully placed in the trunk wrapped and ready to transport to Arizona. The gifts Mom bought for all us New Mexico folks are wrapped and waiting patiently for the tree to be put up. Until then they are taking up all of Cathy's guest room.

Another tough moment was when I was carefully selecting the Christmas Eve presents. Each year everyone gets to open one gift on Christmas Eve. It is always pajamas. This is well thought out because when my kids were bitties I wanted them to be adorable in new jammies for the Christmas morning photos. Mussy hair is acceptable while ratty pjs are not. These gifts always go in the same Nativity gift bags year after year. I bought a bunch of extras to accommodate our growing brood. I was fine while picking the ladies' and grandkids' jammies. When I got to my sons, I realized I was only going to be buying two instead of three this year. I know I didn't buy Ry jammies last year either, but it is still hard. While shopping I kept seeing things that would be perfect for him; if only he was still here with us.

I rest assured that he is with his Heavenly Father, and I don't ever worry about my son. But this mother's heart misses him. I miss him for all of us who loved him but especially for his wife and daughter who lost the most.

The joy I have as I write today is knowing that we have another day to all be together. Today my four daughters went to get pedicures and manicures together and came into our house laughing together with faces full of smiles and companionship. My mom and I stayed here and took care of her great grandkids and my grands. Oh, the sacrifices we make! Little did they know that staying here playing with the kids and knowing they were all enjoying each other gave Mom and me the most joy.

In Him,
Joyful

Nana's Kitchen

SUNDAY, DECEMBER 4, 2011

My Son; I Cry, I Smile

He's my son. Today was tough at church as they did a skit of a son dying
and used the song, "My Son". I couldn't stay. I ran out of church and just
kept running until a sweet friend stopped me and held me in her arms.

God knows exactly how I feel because He watched His own son die for all of us.

Yesterday, I stayed on the couch when I wanted to be out in the beautiful falling snow watching the light parade with my children and grandchildren representing their churches. But I am trying to be honest with myself about what I can and cannot do right now.

Grief is overwhelming me.
I cry not only for myself but for Aunt Judy who lost Uncle Billy a year ago.
I cry for all of us who won't hug our loved ones again on this earth.
I cry for those who are still terrified by the choices their loved ones are making.
I cry for my children who don't have their brother.
I cry for all those who are walking alone through life who don't reach out to Christ who is right beside them.
I cry for my husband whose shoulders shake with his grief at losing his precious son.

God, please comfort us in this joyous, yet emotional season. I smile that we had the opportunity to have Ryan in our lives.
I smile that Dorothy and Elissa are ours because of Ryan's love for them.
I smile that we can lay our lives on Christ and never walk alone.
I smile because I am able to cry and be comforted by those who love me.
I smile because I know I will see my son again.
I smile because God knows where we are headed even when we don't.

But today I know it is okay to cuddle up with my box of tissues and just cry.

In Him,
Joyful

WEDNESDAY, DECEMBER 7, 2011

Crocheting My Blues Away

My crocheting emotion meter is the most accurate at detecting how I am doing. When I am overwhelmed with stress there is no way I could pick up a crochet hook. On the other hand, if I am content and calm I don't crochet either. It is when I am mildly bonkers that I get a lot of projects done.

Of course since this activity is primarily a strategy to maintain mental health I don't do anything fancy or complicated.

Crocheting for me is simply going back and forth with a high-low stitch that results in scarves or blankets only. My elf-like instructional assistant makes hats and other items with all kinds of complicated stitches. If I have to think too much it isn't relaxing or therapy. So I keep it simple!

Last night was our last sign language class and afterward we went shopping. It was frigid cold, but we were motivated to spend for some reason. I found some wonderful yarns for only a dollar a skein. If I get complicated yarn maybe it will look like I learned a new stitch or improved my skills. If I maintain my stress level I may have a couple scarves to pop in the box to my nieces in Seattle.

Crocheting is something I love, but it also gives me a mood reading. What is your mood reader? Eating, shopping, sewing and playing an instrument are all outlets that help us cope with life when the road gets rocky. I pray each of you can enjoy the holidays and manage the heartaches in whatever way heals you best.

In Him,
Joyful

SUNDAY, DECEMBER 18, 2011

Miss You, Ryan

I am missing my son, Ryan, this holiday season. I thank God for Ryan's faith and my knowledge that he is safe in Christ's arms.

In Him, *Joyful*

MONDAY, FEBRUARY 6, 2012

Humbled By Her Words

Losing our son was the hardest thing we could ever live through. Yet God has placed amazing relationships in our lives as a result of who Ryan was. We have been blessed with the love and support of those who loved him. Freedom honored us with her words and her love. The gift of our Ryan keeps blessing us even after his death.

Barb and Ron Barber

A very happy new year to you. I have but one wish for you both for 2012. I pray that God gives you back tenfold the amazing love, happiness and strength that you have given out to everyone that knows you. I have never in my life met two people with hearts as big as yours. You always put others first, even when the shadows seemed to linger in your life. You have always been kind, honest and welcoming. You two have something special inside you, something amazing that radiated not just from Ryan but from all the Barber family. You have put your fingerprint on the hearts of those around you and I am so PROUD to call you FAMILY. May God bless you and yours this new year!

love you always,

freedom

In Him,

Joyful

TUESDAY, FEBRUARY 14, 2012

Any and Every Heart Will Do

My Ryan always gave me heart rocks. He would carry them in his pocket until we were together and then pull one out and smile. My first heart rock was given to me when he was four with a big proud hug. The last one was a couple months before he died when he came for what was to be his last visit. Now my kiddos at school find me heart rocks and are just as tickled as Ry was when they present their treasures. I have been the lucky recipient of pictures of chicken nugget hearts, puddles on the sidewalk hearts, a heart-shaped strawberry and so many other hearts found in the most wonderful places.

Today on Valentine's Day I am believing that a snow heart I saw was heaven sent from my son to his mom who misses him with every breath. Enjoy spending time with our Savior, my son. We will be reunited when the time is right, and I will wrap you in my arms. Wonder how many heart rocks you have gathered in heaven for me!

In Him,
Joyful

SUNDAY, FEBRUARY 19, 2012

Jealous of the Angels

Our hearts are breaking for our friends, the Bacas, who said goodbye to their eighteen year old son, Derek, yesterday. Knowing their pain personally from our loss of our precious Ryan reminds us of how blessed we are that our son loved the Lord. Picturing him welcoming Derek up there around the throne makes me smile. Ryan and Derek had so many common interests as well as struggles. Losing a son to suicide is so painful. But remembering the joy they each brought into our lives in the too short years we had them with us helps. I believe that Ry will be around the throne with the other angels welcoming Lorri and Allen's son into the kingdom. But boy, are we all jealous of the angels spending time with our sons.

In Him,   *Joyful*

SUNDAY, FEBRUARY 26, 2012

When Tomorrow Starts Without Me

"When Tomorrow Starts Without Me"
Stacy Claflin

Ron and I came across this poem last night, and it was as if Ryan sat down to have a chat with us. Losing our son has been unbearable, but there have been blessings as well. We no longer have to worry about him because we rest in the truth that he is safe in God's arms. Another blessing for us is that we have been allowed, through Facebook, to see our compassionate son through the eyes of all those who knew and loved him. That he spent his short time on this earth unselfishly encouraging others just reminds us of what we already know about who Ryan was, and how he lived his life. His struggles with substances and depression were not what defined him. His ability to put others first was what showed his heart. Tomorrow indeed is starting without him physically with us, but he will forever live on in our hearts and memories.

In Him,
Joyful

TUESDAY, FEBRUARY 28, 2012

March 2nd, Ryan Shared His Birthday With Dr. Suess

Ryan's birthday is Friday. He shares it with Dr. Suess and should be celebrating his twenty-six years of life with us. Today I found a sweet, pink heart shaped rock on my walk. I just know Ryan smiled and wished he had placed it in my hand. Oh, how I am missing my son. I can still hear his little, three year old voice squealing, "My birfday March second; my birfday March second." Ironic that we had his goodbye celebration in the same fellowship hall/roller skating rink at our church where he

celebrated so many joyful childhood birthday parties.

Two weeks ago Ron and I went to another goodbye service for another broken teen. Sunday I went to lunch with a sweet senior in high school who should be carefree and looking forward to her future. Instead she continues to grieve her brother who hung himself from the basketball rim in his backyard where he spent countless hours shooting hoops. What are we going to do to stop the loss of life among our young people? The pain of parents, siblings and friends who just keep losing those they love. The stress that these youth are under is literally killing them.

We need to be on our knees for these precious children. It is not enough to be praying unceasingly. We need to be praying with them as we hold both their hands and bring our Christ in the middle of our relationships. Knowing that they are not alone is what having a parent, sibling or friend who is willing to place Christ in the middle of their love and relationship is key. The loneliness and hopelessness can only be wiped away with His unconditional love.

Love is patient. Love is kind. Love isn't jealous. It doesn't sing its own praises. It isn't arrogant. (1 Corinthians 13:4)

There is an urgency to spread God's love. Hope in the truth that He loves us and only wants us to be in a relationship with Him. It is not about religion. It is about a Father that loves us no matter what we do or who we are.

Just as I am, without one plea,
but that thy blood was shed for me,
and that thou bidst me come to thee,
O Lamb of God, I come, I come. (Hymn, Charlotte Elliott)
In Him,   *Joyful*

WEDNESDAY, FEBRUARY 29, 2012

I Am Not Okay With Any Of This

This may not make sense. I have had a bit to drink which is not something I do. But I am so weary with my job, the loss of my son and the worries for my children that I needed an escape. My heart keeps repeating the same thing in this state of vulnerability. My failures as a mother. My failures as a mother. My failures as a mother. Why is my son dead when so many mothers will never have to feel the heartache of losing a child? What could I have done differently? Oh, so many mistakes that can't even be described. Then there is the fact that my remaining three children have little or no relationship with each other. My hope and prayer for having four children no matter what it took was so that they would not have to walk through this life alone. But that has not happened. My three kids seem like they would be just fine if none of the others existed. Oh, believe me they all mourn the death of their brother, Ryan. But none of them take time to reach out to each other. This is one of my greatest failures. That my children do not want and need to be with each other. I am heartbroken and discouraged. Where did I go wrong? What could I have done differently? I see other families whose kids are each other's best friends. Why can't that be mine? Even after losing Ryan that they don't cling to each other baffles me.

I know this is my failure. I didn't bind them together or teach them that they have each other and that is incredibly important. Oh God, how I regret how I treated my kids and all the mistakes I made. I showed them selfishness when I should have shown them compassion. I would say I would like a do over, but the truth is I am pretty sure I would mess that up again.

There is a part of me that feels like the biggest fraud when people speak of how kind and loving I am. What I see in the mirror is a self centered, lazy person with priorities that need serious adjustment. Why else would my son be dead? Why else would my kids not love to be a part of each other's lives? I wish I was who people believe me to be. The reality is that I am broken. I can't do this on my own. The weariness of Ryan's birthday and his unnecessary death are more than I can bear.

Yes, I have had too many glasses of wine. But I am tired. It is not just the wine but life that has zapped me. I am working my ass off at school to help the students in my charge. Instead of appreciation I have parents who condemn my efforts. The feeling of being a wrung out sock is real for me tonight. Tomorrow I must face parent conferences and put the old chin up. What I want to do is toss in the towel and say I give up. I am not the teacher I should be. You are right, you win. I want to give up on my kids and tell them that I will never be able to make it matter to them that they are blessed with each other. What a precious gift they are wasting not clinging to each other. Tonight I am finished.

I know tomorrow is another day and I will climb out of this funk and get back to it. But tonight I am too low to try for even one more minute. My son should be having a birthday. My love of my students should be clear to their parents. My children should be best buds. But life is what life is.

So tomorrow I will blog the joyful thoughts. But for tonight this all just sucks!

In Him,
Joyful, or soon to be Joyful again

FRIDAY, MARCH 2, 2012

Today I Was Blessed, Today I Am Blessed

Halibut - Homer Alaska

My life is blessed. Today, I celebrate not the losses in my life but the blessings. My heart's desire was to have four children and a husband who adored me. Through the generous hearts of four courageous birth moms I was blessed with exactly the children God meant me to share my life with. My husband has been my best friend and heartthrob since I was sixteen years old. Indeed I am blessed.

Life is not always happy. Heartaches come. Some of

these rough times I brought on myself with my choices. Some were just the way life unfolded. Even through the sad or angry times I have never been alone. God is my stretcher when I need Him to be and rejoices with me when life exceeds my wildest dreams.

This family that I am blessed with has traveled all over in our old camper van. From Key West, the southeastern most tip of our country, to the Arctic Circle, the northwestern most point, we have enjoyed every mile. The proof of how joy filled our journeys came at the end of our two month trip to Alaska when we got to the last day and the kids and parents were all wishing for *just one more night*. Mind you, life in a nineteen foot 1975 camper can get a little snug when we cram four kids, two parents and a grandma inside. But the coziness of it warms my heart. We cooked, slept, laughed and pranked each other in those tight quarters. In two months we only rented a hotel room once, and that was because it was pouring rain and we stopped too late to set up camp. Oh, the memories we have to smile about from those trips.

So today on my son's birthday that we are celebrating without him, I am choosing to reflect on the blessings my family has brought to my life. Sitting here at fifty-five having lived the life I have lived and knowing what I know, I would not change a thing. Life unfolds, Christ walks beside me, and I know with all that I am that I have enjoyed the moments and people who are a part of my journey.

Ryan lived life, loved life and knew he was loved unconditionally. Life from today forward will be different without my son in it, but my future holds the joy of all the others that love me and allow me to love them.

Friends, family and my loving husband are here, and I plan to wallow in the blessing of having each of them in my life.

In Him,
Joyful

SATURDAY, MARCH 3, 2012

Send Up a Balloon and a Smile

Oh, what a day; oh, what a day! Wait, that is Shel Silverstein, not Dr. Suess! But really it was a wonderful day for Ryan and Dr. Suess' birthday. Facebook took tribute to Ryan and exploded it among so many who love and loved my son. **Send up a balloon.** A simple idea, but incredible when people all across Facebook and across this country catch the idea and join in.

So yesterday we sent up balloons, some with handwritten messages and some just drifting skyward. Everyone wants it to become a yearly hug among all of us who miss my son who encouraged us all. Next year we will post pictures of the launches to further connect us on his birthday.

Friends brought balloons for us to send up; bright, colorful balloons. This morning our family is gathering for breakfast, and I will bring the twenty-six balloons plus cards, markers and tape to attach their loving words. Smartphones will capture the moment for Elissa and Dorothy who can't be here today. However, they sent up their own balloons yesterday and sang Happy Birthday to her daddy. Again I thank God for my daughter-in-love and granddaughter. What a gift they are in our lives. Balloons and this idea make me look forward to March 2nd in the future. People's hearts and participation in this touch me so. **Happy Birthday Ryan, Dr. Suess, Kylah, Megan and Lisa.**

In Him,

Joyful

SUNDAY, APRIL 22, 2012

Tear Filled Memories

We just have to be thankful for all the ways these memories connect us to our loved ones. Countless situations in life remind us of the times we had with Ryan. He touched everyone he met with his life and his love. Until we see him again, we will smile and cry at all the times we shared and the ones that now have a hole where his presence should be.

In Him,

Joyful

THURSDAY, JUNE 21, 2012

You Remind Me Of Him

A couple of times I have run into a young man who reminded me so much of my sweet Ryan. The other day I met Cisco, a guy who not only looks like Ry, but walked like him and even knew Ryan. Talking to him was comforting. He had similar mannerisms to my son. This guy knew Ryan because of the connections they both had due to their struggles with addiction. When we parted he gave me a quick hug. Hmmmm, it was like absorbing a bit of my son. I have to say I wanted to ask him if I could buy him a Christmas gift since there is a hole in my heart when I see something I want to get for Ryan.

In Him,
Joyful

SUNDAY, OCTOBER 28, 2012

It Is The Truth, and It Is Okay

Sometimes each of us just needs a break. Some would question my need for a day off since teachers like me get the summer off. But believe me, there is a need for a mini vacation here. So I am taking Natalie to the airport as my excuse to spend a couple nights and a day off with Pat. Even one day off seems like a lifeline when I go hang out at Pat's. Her house is just a second home without the chores and with a bonus of a supportive ear and great food.

This weekend we went to dinner with some of Ron's coworkers. As soon as we walked through the door one of them gave me a warm hug and began to tear up. She told me how sorry she was about us losing our son, Ryan. She lost a son who was only a year older than Ry at twenty-five years old. Somehow this new friend gave me permission to grieve. She is still aching fifteen years after her loss and recognizes that it is okay to not be okay forever. Of course we are living, but there is a constant hole in our hearts. I knew that. I live that. But too often I try to just buck up and apologize for not being okay.

This week has been hard. I ran across Ry's cremation bill, death  certificate and his personal effects. Cowardly me took them to a friend's house and left them on her table unable to look at them or even have them in my house. This hit me so hard I couldn't even talk to Ron about it. So much for cleaning and organizing our room.

Thinking back to the dreaded April two and a half years ago, I should have and could have taken more time. Ron and I both only took two weeks off. Crazy! If someone would have told me one of my kids would die by suicide I would have sworn I would never be able to work or breathe again. But at the time I felt guilty for taking that much time off. Well, Ann, who I just met last night, told me to be more honest. She said to be more honest with others and myself. It is okay to not be okay. It is the truth that right now I am not okay. It isn't April or the 5th of the month, but I am missing my loving, crazy Ry.

That is the truth, and it is okay.
In Him,
Joyful

SUNDAY, NOVEMBER 4, 2012

Thankful Even For Tears

Today I am thankful for my tears. In church, Pastor Steve had us share a fond memory of someone we loved who was no longer living. I would love to say I told others how Ryan touched people with his love and encouragement. Instead, I had to leave the sanctuary and roam around sobbing. I wound up in the fellowship hall that is also a roller skating rink. My kids had birthday parties in this space, and we had Ryan's final goodbye party there. I just sat there with tears streaming down my face.

Ron came and found me, and we just hugged and wept over the loss of our son. I am thankful for our tears because we wouldn't be crying without being blessed with twenty-four years of Ryan in our family. The tears are proof of how much he touched our lives and our hearts.

Sometimes it is easy to just move through life, and other times my grief for my son stops me in my tracks. I am getting better at just embracing the tears and memories. I know that his presence in my life as well as his abrupt death will always bring tears of joy and pain.

In Him,
Joyful

WEDNESDAY, NOVEMBER 14, 2012

Ryan is Safe

Thankful for my Ryan up in heaven. Yesterday, I found out another mom is terrified and heartbroken with the reality that she doesn't know where her son is. He has disappeared. The two rescue dogs that were most important to him were left alone in his apartment to starve. His mother's heartache is not from the fact that he is front page news as a heartless animal killer, but that whatever is broken in him that caused him to leave must be monumental. The judging of her son will fade, but his own safety and the unknown are impossible.

I feel almost guilty and lucky that Ryan is gone. Not that I would ever choose to have my son take his life. The pain and worry of where he is and how he is are over. Never again do I have to go through losing him. My grief is still real and the emptiness of living without him in this life is unbearable. But the saying goodbye is behind me along with the coming to terms with reality.

My prayers are with this family and all the families who can't get in touch with their children. The not knowing, the worry of what if, the fear of the brokenness being too great to bear is all consuming. I don't envy them. I pray for them to have the strength, the courage and the knowledge that

Denali, Alaska~Cameron, Ryan and their adventurous dad

depression and drug abuse are greater than our love sometimes. My greatest blessing is that my son shared his faith, and I know he rests in Christ's arms even as my arms ache to hold him. I have not been haunted by all the what ifs that could turn my precious memories to guilt. Nor have I been terrorized by images of his death but have been gifted with memories of his smile that lit up his eyes.

Today I am thankful for the hardest reality of my life and the love I still cling to of my son.

In Him,
Joyful

THURSDAY, MARCH 14, 2013

Even For Suicide

I am grateful even for the circumstances of my son's suicide.

~He died in Colorado, so I won't be driving past that tragic place.

~He blessed us with our daughter-in-love, Dorothy.

~His daughter, Elissa, is a gift he left for us to enjoy. It brings a smile when she gets one of his expressions, tilts her head like him or gets his goofy look in her eye.

~Others that loved my son have become family to me. He has increased the love in my heart where I thought there would be a void.

~Opportunities. Ryan's death has put me in the position to comfort other mothers, families and friends in their hardest hours.

~Joy. As I watch him in videos and listen to him on voicemail I hear the love he had for me and am comforted that he knew he was loved.

~Proof. Ryan's sudden death gave me proof that by clinging to my faith I have the strength to get through any of life's hardships. Proof that I never walk alone. Proof that God is my stretcher, and I can lay my whole life on Him.

There are mothers who live with a reminder of their child's death even in their own homes. There are mothers who don't have a daughter-in-love or grandchild to hold. There are mothers who don't have a husband that took hours of video as their kids were growing up. There are mothers who are suffering a loss that is fresh, raw and unbearable today. My prayers and heart are with them.

Don't get me wrong. I would take this truth away if I could. Bring him back into our world so I could cling to him. That is not possible. So I rest in the truth that he is safe in a place where I am promised to be myself someday. The reality of his death and my aching will be a part of me from that day forward. Losing a child is a horrific experience no matter the circumstance. It truly is an amputation of the heart.

~Hope. I have hope that God uses all things for good. I have evidence that Ryan's life mattered, and his death brought people together in love. **Faith, Friends and Family.** For these I am grateful.

In Him,
Joyful

TUESDAY, MARCH 26, 2013

Gently Worn Bible

Whether life is in that magical, everything-is-going-perfect season,
or life has brought a violent storm, life is better when
our Bible and prayer are at the center.

There is a saying when Christ is your center the circumference takes care
of itself. As I enter the next week, I feel myself bracing for anguish.
I need to focus on the blessings of Ryan's life instead of the agony of his
death.
Falling apart is not necessary.
But when I grieve Jesus has me wrapped in His arms.
So I will pick up His word, put down my computer and trust Him with
my heartbreak.
His gift to me is the simple fact that I have not spent a day worrying
about my son since he left
my world to make Jesus his home.
He is safe.
We will be together again.

In Him,
Joyful

WEDNESDAY, MARCH 27, 2013

Post From Day After Suicide Changed My Family 4-6-10

Life will never be quite the same after today. My precious, tormented son took his own life. How can this be? Only faith and our relationships will get us through this heartbreak. Numb, crushed, unable to breathe are a few ways people described their ache. God, you must cradle him in your arms for me now.

Never again will I pick up the phone and hear, "Hello, Beautiful!" I can't stop calling his phone to hear his voice on the other end. This voice that was forever silenced on April 5th. Parents should never have to make arrangements like this. Our kids are supposed to lay us to rest, not the other way around.

God performed a miracle for me the night before I lost my son. I met a cousin of my friend, Jenn, and actually had dinner with her Sunday night after Jenn's surgery. Years ago, her son took his life. I asked her how she possibly survived such a loss. She said it so simply, "By faith."

No big mystery. Just have a continuous, personal relationship with Jesus Christ.

Unbelievably, not even twenty-four hours later I was faced with the untimely loss of my son. It has been an amazingly long day. "By faith" my family is making it through. Looking at pictures, reliving memories and a whole lot of time spent holding loved ones hands and kneeling before our Awesome God. This house has not seen prayer of this magnitude in far too long. Good news is, we are putting God at the center of all of this

Ryan is resting in God's faithful arms tonight, and I am managing a peaceful loneliness while surrounded by my family and friends.

There are already countless blessings from Ryan's death as we all come together to celebrate his life. Hope he in some way knows how very much he touched so many.

In Him,
Joyful but lonely

Reposted almost three years later just to remind myself and others of God's faithfulness in even our darkest moment.
I can do all things through Christ who strengthens me (Phil. 4:13)

MONDAY, APRIL 1, 2013

Beyond Procrastination

"If it weren't for the last minute, I would never get anything done."

Procrastination. Now that is something I am extremely good at. Ron and I just finished our taxes last night. Okay, I realize that it is only April first, and they are not due until April fifteenth, so that doesn't seem like the last minute. But the truth is we just finished our 2010 taxes. Don't panic! We are not in jail yet. Now you are thinking this is not the last minute, but years overdue. You are right.

But the truth is, we could not get past these taxes. They represent our lives before Ryan died. There are receipts in this pile for cremation, suits to attend a funeral for a son and a brother, money we gave him to buy a plane ticket to come home only a month before he took his life.

The before and after of April 5, 2010 are dramatic as our life shifted from having our son, Ryan, in our earthly lives and living with the heartbreak of his death. Every time we sat down to tackle the paperwork of taxes for 2010 we disintegrated into tears and put it all away.

Well, thankfully that pile of receipts and all the little boxes on all the government forms are finally completed, and we can send them off and throw them in the file cabinet. I wish we could have put this behind us years ago, so we wouldn't have had it weighing on our minds for so long. But we all do what we can when we can.

Time to write a note to the IRS to put in the big envelope to explain. Time to forgive ourselves for making the last minute years past when it should have been. Time to accept that Ryan won't be calling again to bring me his latest recipe success or call me *"**Beautiful Mom**"*.
Time to treasure the memories and people in our lives.
Time to cling to faith, family and friends as we journey through this week

that is our son's departure week. April fifth is the day he took his life, but he didn't take our love or memories of him.

In Him,
Joyful

FRIDAY, APRIL 5, 2013

3 years, 1095 days, 26,280 hours Feels Like a Lifetime Without My Son

Three years, 1095 days, 26,280 hours without my son. No wait; 24 years, 8794 days, 211,056 hours of life with my son. This is a day to celebrate not his death, but his outstanding life. Ryan was a gift to all of us, and though he is not walking the earth any longer, his love and encouragement continues to be a force in our lives.

Ryan was a unique person who could and would make anyone feel like they were his most favorite of all. Ron and I have heard so many say that Ry was their best friend. How can that be? Most people only have one best friend. But you know each of them is right. Ryan had more best friends than most of us have casual friends. There was just something about that guy that made people feel accepted and valued. If only we could bottle his personality to dispense to others the world would be a more accepting place.

This is a day that I celebrate the life of my son and grieve that I no longer get to pick up the phone and hear him call me beautiful. I was beautiful to Ryan; we all were. He saw past the physical and emotional scars to the person that was worth knowing. Bringing out the best in others was as simple as breathing for this man.

Now I know Ry was not perfect, in fact far from it. He never believed in himself as much as he believed in those around him. I only pray that now that he is home in heaven he is clear about the impact his words and love had on each of us. Ryan tended to look at his mistakes rather than his accomplishments. That is so sad to me.

JJ Heller wrote, *"not for what i have done, or what i will become, who'll love me for me?"* Ryan loved others and was tolerant of people's oddities. What a treasure to have that outlook in life. Not to always be jealous or condemning of others but to encourage and sing others' praises is the way we should all live.

We are spending today reflecting on the happy times spent as a family with our son. Bet I will find a perfect heart rock and know he would have picked it up and handed it to me with a smile if only he could.

In Him,
Joyful

SATURDAY, APRIL 27, 2013

Gratitude in a Dream

I had a dream of Ryan last night. It was both wonderful and horrible. I so appreciate that I got to spend a couple hours on the phone with him the day he left. Thankful I wasn't doing my usual micromanaging mom thing that day.

In this dream, I knew he was going to die, and I clung to him. We all did. My whole family was there. Each of us was tortured to let him walk away. No hug was enough, no gazing into his eyes was enough, no smelling him was enough, knowing it was the last. So though I would love one more hug, this dream made me blessed for the times I had and not jealous for that one more moment with him. I am grateful for the times I had and cherish my incredible memories.

In Him,
Joyful

But, as it is written: *What no eye has seen, nor ear heard, nor the heart of man imagined, what God has prepared for those who love him.* (1Corinthians 2:9)

SUNDAY, JUNE 16, 2013

Heavenly Father's Day Celebration

Ryan, we have Lissa here for Father's Day. We will share videos and pictures and stories of you. Wish you were here to get her great big hugs. She is making a card for her Papas and Hector. You would have loved seeing the energetic, inquisitive almost nine year old that she is today. We will keep your love for her alive here until you meet again decades from now. Wish you could know how your love and encouragement has impacted all our lives, my son. I am so grateful that a huge piece of you lives on in Lissa's big brown eyes and incredible (sometimes ornery) smile.

You left too soon, but you left behind an unimaginable bond between all of us who love you, Ry. Since your sudden trip home so many other families have lost their sons, daughters, brothers, sisters, grandkids and cousins to suicide. Right now I know of three families holding their breath and praying their young adult children can get through the darkness without making that irreversible decision. Some say my pain is greatest because I am your mom. The reality is suicide impacts everyone you loved and that loved you equally. The joy you left behind is greater than the ache of losing you, but I still wish we could have a "do over" and be together today and into the future. God knows, I haven't worried about you a day since you left. You are wrapped in His presence, but I am jealous and want you in my presence and my arms much longer than the twenty-four years you were here.

Until we meet again, we will do what you did and encourage others, reach out to those who have the overwhelming loss that changes life and keep our love for you always in Lissa's life.

Hearts to you and Happy Father's Day, Mom,
Joyful

WEDNESDAY, FEBRUARY 19, 2014

My Father, Not My Master

"Servants can only bring others to a master. Sons are the ones who can point others to their Father." By: Jack Frost's *Homecoming*

This really touches my heart. I try so hard not to be Martha with tasks to complete, but Mary who can sit without guilt at Jesus' feet. One of my greatest concerns about retirement is that I will have free time and feel guilt rather than pleasure at relaxing into it. It is sad that our self worth gets so caught up in accomplishments instead of relationships. This is a stronghold that I need to shatter.

Today, my sweet mom is having a busy day. She is taking her dog to the groomer and going to play cards with her friends. It is natural to be crazy with schedules when we have kids at home and careers. What is hard is the transition from a house full of schedules to just the two of us with less on our calendar. I am reading a book by Jack Frost: *Embracing Father's Love*. I am learning so much about myself and how I value my servant self more than my relationship self.

Since we lost Ryan, I have holed up and done very little socializing. I was such a social person before this heartbreak. Ron has been wonderful getting me out there for Saturday morning breakfasts with other couples. Left to my own, I am content being home alone. Today, I sit here writing this while other staff are laughing and conversing over an extended lunch. Home is my comfort zone but also my self imposed prison.

It is up to me to continue praying for God to show me a way to get back into ministry and off my couch. Then I have to be willing to take a risk and move into relationships once again. I never thought that I would be someone so frightened of connecting with others. My Father knows, and I just need to rest in that and let Him be my Dad.
In Him,
Joyful

SATURDAY, MARCH 29, 2014

Special Heartfelt Message~A Year Old But Still Special

We got this generous message a year ago on Ryan's Going Home Day. It has now been almost four years since Ryan left us. His death day is right between my birthday and Natalie's. Such mixed emotions this week of the year. Tearful gratitude for getting the opportunity to love Ryan and my other precious children. There are so many people that have become family because of our kids and our community. How truly blessed we are even in grief.

I've been thinking about you a lot lately. It seems like such a long time since I saw you last. I was thinking about your mom and dad and your brothers and sister the other day and they are awesome. Rock solid in

their faith and family. Your mom is like the lighthouse of Los Alamos guiding people away from darkness with the light that shines from her heart and soul, your dad is a voice of reason in the chaos. Your brother Cam and his wife and kids are doing amazing things with their faith. Tanner from what I see on FB is going to accomplish great things throughout his life. And Nat has such an amazing gift of compassion and shows her kindness in such an admirable way. And above all of that you have brought so many wonderful people together and so many great and amazing things have happened because of you and the memories we all have of you. Miss you Ryan! Freedom Elliot

TUESDAY, JULY 29, 2014

Trauma Induced Autism

Au·tism

ˈôˌtizəm/

noun

1. a mental condition, present from early childhood, characterized by difficulty in communicating and forming relationships with other people and in using language and abstract concepts.

I am blessed to spend my life working with these courageous kids at the middle school level. It is a challenge to find ways to smooth out the challenges they face and provide them with strategies to become more independent and normal feeling as they explore the brilliance of their lives and talents.

Lately, it has occurred to me that Autism, or the characteristics of Autism, doesn't always occur in early childhood. My life and personality have changed since losing my precious son to suicide four years ago. It feels like I am incapable of the life and relationships I had before. Everything seems measured by before and after we lost Ry.

Before

~ I loved being around people.

~I initiated social gatherings.

~I was involved in the Young Life ministry.

~I didn't crave my bed and being alone.

After

~I avoid being around people.

~I have a hard time going to gatherings with a lot of people.

~I crave being alone and spend way too much time in my bed.

Every year I am amazed at the courage of my ASD students as they bravely face life that is so hard to face. They give me strength to venture out even when I want to run the other way. Their challenges are not visible physically but are so real. Grief is the same. Others look at each of us and think we should be fine and wonder at our behaviors. The desire to be normal, fearless and social is there for people with ASD and for those grieving. The good news is I see hope and progress in my middle schoolers all the time. This gives me hope that my personality will keep evolving as well.

In Him,

Joyful

WEDNESDAY, OCTOBER 15, 2014

Final Taxes Filed; a Toast to Our Son

A journey to our *FINAL* tax day!

Of course we will be paying taxes in the future, but today was the day we *FINALLY* finished years of unfiled taxes. Shocking, I know. The truth is after our son took his life over four years ago, we just couldn't face the tax stuff. There were receipts for cremation, the suits and dresses we bought to wear to his funeral, money we had sent to help him out and checks for his birthday gifts. It seemed this big pile of papers held a journey of love, family, sorrow and heartache. Everything was either from before Ry died or after. Even the iPad we stood in line for two days before he died was used days later by his brother to write a eulogy. Birthday gifts and Easter baskets were purchased just before our lives forever changed.

So we let the receipt pile that we couldn't face grow. Last year, an incredible friend hugged us through three years of long overdue taxes. Each of us cried, prayed and hugged our way through the painful mess that we had to face. This year we got the last two years completed. Today for the first time since filing 2008 taxes, we are current on our taxes. God's smile on us is that we even got a sizable refund as we e-filed for the very first time. (Can't e-file overdue taxes)

I feel such relief that this task is behind us. At the same time it makes me realize how God has walked beside us through the waves of grief these past few years. Life will forever be divided between when Ry was here with us, and when he left us that day after Easter four years ago.

Our future receipts will include a mixture of family trips, grandkid's birthday gifts and the occasional tough purchase. Life is full of wonderful memories and hard to face goodbyes that are bound to come. For today, we will enjoy a much awaited celebratory toast to Ryan. The gifts he continues to give us far outweigh the expense of our grief over losing him too soon.

In Him,
Joyful

THURSDAY, MARCH 19, 2015

Wrapped His Trip Home in Our Birthdays

Ryan wrapped his trip home in our birthdays. This April 5th will be five years since my sweet son took his life. Easter is on April 5th this year. My birthday is April 4th and Natalie will be twenty-five on April 6th, Her twentieth birthday was horrific. Enduring the death of her brother at such a young age is unimaginable. Someone graciously went out and bought her a cake that just sat there. No one was hungry for sweets or any food for that matter. We were all just in shock!

For her twenty-first birthday Ron and I took Natalie on a train trip to Santa Barbara. It was just necessary to get out of town! Ron made the trip exciting with his encounter with the Federal Marshall that thought

 he was tracking someone. Then he missed the train in San Bernardino when he got off at a smoke stop. Ron doesn't smoke. We could look at our loss of Ryan on April 5th as devastating our birthdays. Instead, we choose to believe he wrapped his trip home in them. I have ached and been heart sick the past five years missing my son. But I don't worry about him. He accepted and believed. I have no doubt he is in heaven enjoying a closeness with Christ.

Ryan touched so many lives and continues to be alive in our hearts. Just wish I could wrap my arms around his neck. I would probably choke him before I hugged him for all the heartache.

In Him,
Joyful

SATURDAY, MARCH 28, 2015

Step by Step, Day by Day, Month by Month, Year by Year

Almost five years ago our lives were changed forever when our son took his own life. It seems our lives now are measured by before Ryan died, and since Ryan died. For a bit, we could barely function. Oh, we all went to work, paid most of the bills and met with friends for dinner, but there was a numbness that hadn't been there before this loss. Others who were close knew the struggle. Those who barely knew us may have never guessed from the smiles we put on our faces.

Even though we keep moving, grief is still as much a part of our lives as breathing. Since we lost Ryan, Ron and I have watched too many others walk through the pain of losing their children by their own hand. It is always indescribably raw, the moments right after. I have heard some say that this can't be right because they aren't as brave as we are. It isn't courage that gets us through, but faith.

My prayer is always that no other family has to lose a loved one to suicide. But the truth is suicide is too common, so families are affected. Even five years later, I don't know what to say to those who are grieving or those who fear for their children's safety. The right words just don't seem to come.

My prayer is that each of us has a faith that walks us through even the impossible situations of life. That we never feel like we have to face life alone. Others have been here for us, and Ron and I cling to each other, but our faith is what has allowed us to live through this pain. Step by step, day by day, month by month, and now year by year we are moving through life without Ryan in our arms. But he is always in our hearts and so often in our thoughts.

In Him,

Joyful

THURSDAY, JULY 9, 2015

Enough;;;;;;;;;;

Too often we focus on the "what is wrong" and forget to see what is going so well. I know I am guilty of this. It is hard to give myself a break choosing instead to dwell on the hurts in my life.

Jenn said she may get a tattoo that says *enough*. That is so powerful and has such a broad meaning.

I am *enough*~~love myself

I have *enough*~~be satisfied

Others are *enough*~~stop being jealous

There is a movement called the Semicolon Tattoo Project.

Why the semicolon? *"A semicolon is used when an author could've chosen to end their sentence, but chose not to,"* the site said. *"The sentence is your life, and the author is you."*

As most of you know, Ron and I lost our precious son to suicide five years ago. His life should not have ended. He should have chosen to continue. But deep inside his heart he didn't feel *enough*. A friend asked me yesterday if I have been grieving more lately because I have guilt about Ryan's death. Thankfully, I don't have guilt. How much sadder it would be if I felt that I wasn't *enough* or didn't do *enough* to love my son. What matters most is Ryan knew we all loved him unconditionally just as he loved each of us. That is *enough*.

Our loss has given Ron and I the opportunity to be present for others who have ached from the loss of a child. Even in death, Ryan's story, his sentence has not ended. His generous heart has led to treasured relationships that we would not have had without him. Although I believe he should have used the semicolon instead of the gun, my Ryan was *ENOUGH*.

I am beyond thankful I got to be his mom.

In Him,
Joyful

FRIDAY, OCTOBER 23, 2015

Courage to Choose a Different Option

Just like everyone is not meant to be a scientist at NASA, not everyone is meant to be a student at a public school. A teacher told us that Ryan was not having fun at school. How could he? He was lousy at being a student there. That didn't mean he was lousy, just that school was not his path. One of my biggest regrets was not thinking outside the lines and giving him a different path. Ryan was caring, kind, inventive, fun-loving, talented. He had more identities than most.

Snowboarder, chef, fisherman, friend, confidante, encourager, jokester, father, student of life.

When Ryan found an interest he pursued it with his entire being. The Christmas our kids got a unicycle, Ryan spent the whole day outside trying over and over to master it. He concluded that he could succeed if only he knew how to juggle. Hmmm. When his Uncle Mike tried to teach him to water ski Ry was tireless in his efforts to get up. The rest of us just wanted him to give up, but our little man kept telling his uncle to "hit it" one more time. Ryan was not a school student. School seemed impossible to him. He didn't have the academic skills, so he acted out. Who would want to face twelve years of failure? Every day teachers hand you back the red ink proof that you failed once again. Could he have tried harder? Yep.

But the reality is that he didn't fit there. Not breaking with the norm and getting my precious son out of school remains my biggest regret in life. Our schools work for the majority of our kids. But there are those who are looking at years of torturous failure unless their parents have the courage to find a better path for them. Ryan would have flourished in Project Based Learning where he could have had hands-on experiences to grasp difficult concepts. The best he ever did with academics was when he was tutoring younger kids. He felt like an Einstein when he helped much younger kids. His eyes shined in a way that never happened in a classroom. This is difficult for me to write; difficult to admit. I applaud those parents who homeschool, charter school or find the path that works for their young ones. I wish I had been less of a rule follower with my own son. My hope is that others who still have the chance seize the opportunity and let their kids flourish without a public education decade plus sentence.

In Him, *Joyful*

FRIDAY, NOVEMBER 20, 2015

Accepting Me Every Day

I am so thankful we have your voice and laugh recorded, so I can just breathe in the sound of you. Each picture and video gives me a chance for a visit with who you are, who you were and the love you had for others.

There are moments when life occurs, and I just need to pick up the phone and hear you on the other end. Will there ever come a day I can take your phone number out of my contact list? I tell myself it is okay to leave it there even though a different voice would answer if I pressed send.

I see you in others around me. Some that are a part of your story, and some who just have something that seems familiar. Others' generosity reminds me of you. When I see someone take time to lift others up, you are right there in front of me.

Too often now life moves along without you in my daily thoughts. This breaks my heart. Guilt wells up in me at how easy it is to get caught up. Suddenly in a quiet moment a thought turns to you and my breath catches. That is when you are right there with me, in my heart.

How fortunate I am to have others in my life who share my love and my loss. I am comforted by their understanding of how different life is without you. Truth is I am who I am today because you were here but also because you are gone. My loss is such a large part of who I am. It takes time, but I am trying to be comfortable in this new skin that is me. I have to learn to love this new me. No longer do I surround myself with others, spend time out and about, but am alone so much more. It is still difficult accepting that I don't engage in life like I used to. Accepting me and letting me be me is vital. Beating myself up for not reaching out will not serve me. Better to let my life unfold from here and enjoy who I am today.

I am not who I was, but this is still me; the new me.
Do I miss you? Every day.

In Him,
Joyful

SATURDAY, FEBRUARY 27, 2016

Ryan Connections Make Us Family

My Son,

This is a difficult week for your family, especially your precious little girl. Lissa and I spoke last night, and she asked if it would be alright if she waited on sending up your birthday balloons. You see she just lost her Gramma Sheila and will be consumed with the goodbye process this week. Her service is Friday, two days after your birthday. Our sweet Lissa sounded overwhelmed. Too many heartaches for an eleven year old.

You would have been thirty this year, my son. It is hard to think that you left almost six years ago. Even today, you remain such a big piece of our hearts. Little things catch me off guard and remind me of you. Just the other day I had to sit down as I heard a laugh that sounded exactly like yours. We may not be able to wrap our arms around you, but we carry you with us always.

One of the most important truths for me is that I have not been angry with either you, me or God in the face of this. I don't lay awake at night wondering what if, could I have, why did he, if only. I have been blessed with a peace about how life unfolded. Would I change it if I could? Absolutely!

I guess what I need you to know is there is no need for forgiveness between us. There is no thought that there was selfishness when this happened. There is only sadness that you are not here to telephone and say, "Hello, Beautiful." The biggest regret is that your precious little girl doesn't get to know you and learn life from your encouraging perspective. You see, even with the choices that you made in your life the ones that matter most are the ones that keep you forever in each of our hearts and thoughts. The lesson you taught us was to encourage others.

There are people in my life that I will never meet in person. People who are my online family because you lifted them. Some you only met a time or two, but each is still family because of your connection with them. If we can gift Lissa one thing from her daddy it needs to be to love others as you loved. I pray she can remain other-focused and not self-focused as her life unfolds with so much of you in her. I wish you could see her, Son. She is bright, determined, inquisitive, creative and loving.
Lissa is a gift.

Tears are falling, and my heart is full. I love you. I miss you. I am so thankful that you are and will always be a part of our lives. God showed us through you that family are those who we fold into our hearts. Family can happen so quickly. It is not how long we know others, but how we are touched by them that makes us family. Son, you are so many things: father, brother, fisherman, chef, artist, snowboarder, friend, son, surfer, encourager, connector, **Angel.**

In Him,
Joyful

MONDAY, FEBRUARY 29, 2016

Ryan's 30th, Still a Celebration

Do everything in love. (1 Corinthians 16:14)

Grace and Monique found heart rocks on their beach walk and thought of me. Grace is including me in her family from far away. Monique wondered which one I would like best. That is easy, her heart for others. Her heart for me. The love you show me is everything. I get through the storms of life by the love of others.

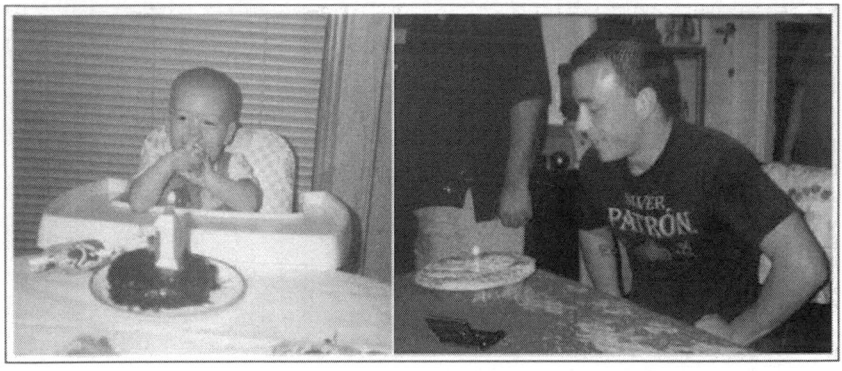

This morning I had a sad dream and woke up wondering how I was going to make it through this week of Ryan's birthday. As I sat down with coffee to check Facebook your love just poured off the page and filled my heart.

G

WEDNESDAY, MARCH 2, 2016

Thanks For the Memories, My Son

Happy Birthday, Scooter!

Today would have been your thirtieth birthday, and we should be teasing you about being an old man. But you, my son, will be forever young. We won't be watching your hair turn grey or thin, your beer belly grow or hear about your aches and pains. You will remain twenty-four in our eyes forever.

I have spent the past few days tearfully looking at pictures and videos. Just listening to your voice makes me smile. My heart aches for you to bring me one of your delicious, creative recipes. For your last birthday Dad and I gave you a fly tying kit and a book called *Writing Cookbooks For Dummies*. On your death certificate I got to fill out I listed you as a *chef* because in our eyes and your heart you were one. You were so much more than that. Your most important role was encourager. My heart would dance when I picked up the phone and heard you say, "Hello, Beautiful". I think you saw the beauty in all of us. There are people like Jess Bailey who still write on your wall that you only met once. Others like Paul Smith you grew up with and are forever in his heart.

Ryan, I don't know what birthdays in heaven are like, but if there is a way to turn it into a party you will. Rex will be up there celebrating not only you but his sweet Megan's twenty-first. My son, you are my heart. You have been since the first time I met you. You will be when I am old and losing my memories. I am gifted with memories and having your Dorothy and Lissy to love. Your family has grown with Hector and Ami to give me even more to love.

Happy Birthday, Son. Today we celebrate your life with a balloon launch at Overlook Park where you sped around on your bicycle. The joy you brought will be there this afternoon along with stories of your adventures. As Bob Hope would say, 'Thanks for the memories."

In Him,
Joyful

THURSDAY, MARCH 3, 2016

Your Love Pours Over Me

I have heard it said that
The best feeling of happiness is when you are happy you have made someone else happy.

Yesterday my day was filled with hugs, balloons, hearts and you letting me know how much I am loved. How much Ryan is loved. How much our family is loved. I hope I show all of you how much your touch means to me, and just how much you are loved.

Let love and kindness be the motivation in all you do.
(1 Corinthians 16:14)
A lifestyle that changes others.
Changes us.
Has the power to change the world one connection at a time.
You drenched me in your love and kindness.
Friends, family, faith.
My life is full.

In Him
Joyful

THURSDAY, SEPTEMBER 8, 2016

Unexpected Celebrity

When a tragedy occurs in our families we get put in the spotlight. The beauty is that communities step forward to embrace us and offer their love and support. The hard part is reliving the grief every time we step out into that community.

Last week a family in our community lost their dad, son and husband unexpectedly. He and his seventh grader were riding bikes to school. His death changed an ordinary day into an extraordinary loss. Instead of football games and soccer practice their weekend was spent in a puddle surrounded by friends and family trying desperately to find the words to ease the un-easable pain. This family's loss reminds each of us of the losses in our own lives. Whether we have lost a parent, sibling, child or friend we relate to the heart numbing pain.

My heart reaches back to losing my son, Ryan, over six years ago. Time passes, but the missing piece of my heart remains. Others hold each other a little tighter recognizing that it could just as easily be their family moving through this pain. Once the service is over and out-of-town guests have gone home, the refrigerator still is full of lovingly made casseroles, but the house feels empty and quiet. Then the reality sinks in that life is forever changed. Just going to the grocery store is hard. In our little town everyone cares, everyone wants to know if you are okay. Everyone wants you to know they are there for you. Unexpected celebrity. You are grateful for the support. But you just can't talk about it anymore.

You just wanted to get out of the house for a moment. I know this sounds harsh, ungrateful even. But for me it was just too hard knowing everyone knew that my heart was broken.

I found myself driving to the next town to get away. Anonymity was what I craved. Eventually life moves on, the tears flow less, and your celebrity fades. Oh, I will forever be the mom whose son took his life. But as time passes, I am also the lady who has a basket of toys for everyone to use at the park, Noni and a retired teacher. Thank God for community.
Thank God for others to wrap their hearts around us.
Thank God even for unexpected celebrity.

Our Lissa all grown up

In Him,
Joyful

FRIDAY, FEBRUARY 17, 2017

Grandgirl, Passports and a New Room

My heart is full and my home is a bit fuller too. Our twelve year old grand girl has come to live with us for middle school. We are enrolling her in an online public school to give us flexibility with her schedule, and so we can be more hands-on with her learning. She is the one who asked to come live with us, and Dorothy and Hector supported her decision. She and I have been busy de~Natalie~ing her room and Lissa~izing it.

Ron and I have a little plaque on our mantle that says, "We love our birdhouse full of birds." That is how we feel about having Lis here. As wonderful as an empty nest is, it is fabulous to have a young one here to love and encourage. The truth is Lissa brings a new life to our home. Her curious enthusiasm to learn and be involved encourages us.

We all sat down and came up with the rules list. She has spent summers with us, so she knows how we live and what we value. There may be bumps in the future. We will be okay as long as we all let each other know what drives us nuts, and what makes us smile.

Wednesday is Thrive aka youth group, so Wednesday night will now be date night for Noni and Papa. Lis already got her first mail at our house from her loving cousin, McKayla. It not only made Lis smile, but she wrote back immediately. I love that my grands are sending each other snail mail. This is another thing that makes me smile

Grandparents raising grandkids is happening more and more. It used to be that we all lived close enough so the grandparents as well as aunts and uncles all raised kids as a community~family. We love that we have this opportunity to love Ryan's daughter. He would be so thrilled with the young lady that Lis is becoming. She has his love for others and his adventurous heart. When I look into her brown eyes I see her dad's heart. She is her own person but got a good bit of the best of both her parents. Having her here gives us the chance to steer her away from the pitfalls her parents made and toward the opportunities that will give her the biggest world possible. Drugs and alcohol and the shame of them took her dad. Our hope is to provide Lis with successes that keep her from repeating his missteps.

She asked for a passport for Christmas, so she could see the world. Guess Ron and I need to get out the map and dust off our own passports. Here

we come, world, with Lissa in the seat right next to us.

In Him,
Joyful

THURSDAY, APRIL 6, 2017

Bittersweet Week

I am thankful others know this week is bittersweet for Cameron, Tanner, Natalie, Ron and me. It is also so hard on Dorothy and Elissa.

This is the week:
Ron and I celebrate my birthday.
Found out we couldn't conceive.
Lost our first chosen son, Logan.
Tanner fell 80 feet off a cliff and broke his back, but survived.
Lost my Grandpa Friedman.
Blessed with our daughter, Natalie.
And painfully said goodbye to our son, Ryan.

Natalie was and is my best birthday present ever. We found out about her the day after my birthday at my grandfather's funeral. She was born the next day. God's timing is impeccable. Cameron, Ryan and Tanner were so excited to be big brothers to this tiny, miracle baby. My heart aches that she had to be

Little League White Rock, New Mexico - July 99

in such pain on her twentieth birthday. That each birthday week we share for the rest of our lives is **bittersweet** with the heartache of missing Ryan.

One of our most precious gifts is that we share the joy and pain of life. That others wish us happy birthday knowing that it is a mix of celebration of life and a heartbreak of death. Losing our son, their brother, nephew, cousin, grandson, her father and so many people's close friend is a defining time in our lives. It brought us together in grief, memory and connected us with each other.

I love this week, and I dread this week.

My Natalie

My Ryan

My Cameron

My Tanner

My family and friends are my most treasured gifts.

In Him,

Joyful

WEDNESDAY, OCTOBER 18, 2017

Joyful, Prayerful, Thankful. It Takes Time to Get There

How is this even possible with the heartaches and heartbreaks that life includes? Be thankful in all things? Thankful for unbearable loss, for excruciating pain, for life's most horrible circumstances? Is that even humanly possible? It seems like a command that is beyond possible. Yet, as we get past the storms in life we get to choose how we move forward with our new realities.

Losing our son to suicide seven years ago seemed like one of the most impossible moments to be thankful for. Don't misunderstand. If we could go back and have our precious son back we would at all costs. But our lives include this loss and always will. That moment forever changed our lives. Nothing will ever be as it was before we lost our Ryan. So with our broken hearts, how are we thankful? Not thankful for our loss but for the opportunity and understanding to reach out and be there for other families going through similar loss. Our prayer is that we don't ever need to use this connection with others, but the reality is that too often over the last seven years we needed to be there to hug, hold onto and understand the grief that is drowning other families.

JOY for us is Jesus first, then Others, then Yourself. It is one of my goals to live my life this way. There is no way we could endure the pain that others are going through on our own. Only walking toward them with prayer and hand in hand with Jesus makes it possible. Others~putting others first always brings us more comfort than we could ever give them. In both putting Jesus in the center and others before ourselves, we actually have healed enough to be grateful for the loss of our son. Not grateful for the loss but for the opportunities his loss has opened for Ron and me. What we are joyful for is that we know that Ryan would be filled with joy that his love and heart for others is continuing even through his death. A pastor said, "Jesus is not my crutch but my stretcher. I don't lean on him but lay my whole life on Him."

I know that we could not have survived the loss of my Ryan without the friends that surrounded us with their love, the family who held us up and Jesus' wrapping us in His arms. Our lives and our hearts will always have a painful tear where Ryan's death tore out this huge hole. Our lives and our hearts have also expanded with the love and connections to others because of our loss.

Our purpose in life is~

To know Him and to make Him known.

To build our relationship with Jesus through prayer and reading His Word/the Bible and to share His love with others. We know that through our loss Ron and I have spent more time in relationship building with Christ and with others who need Him in their lives as they move through their life.

Thankful in Him,

Joyful

In 2018, I blogged~but not about losing my son. I will always miss my son but the loss will not always be my focus and that is okay.

MONDAY, FEBRUARY 25, 2019

Almost March 2nd Once Again

It is almost March 2nd once again. My sweet little Ryan comes to mind running around the house announcing to everyone that his birthday is March 2nd. He so enjoyed his birthdays. What a gift it is to have all the pictures of his enormous smiles behind such a variety of birthday cakes over the years. Each year I miss that I am not spending just one more birthday with my son. Oh, but what treasures all the memories are that I did get to spend with him. My pout is that twenty-four was just not enough.

A gift I do have on each and every March 2nd is the love of so many others that continue to share their hearts for Ryan. He touched so many lives and the memories they carry of him have connected me to them over the years. Connections between those of us who loved him is the gift he left us with. I am beyond grateful for all that send me heart rocks, pictures of hearts or just calls to share a memory of Ry.

Sweet Kylah shares his March 2nd birthday and generously puts an extra candle on her cake every year for Ryan. His birthday twins include some that are so precious to me. Megan shares his birthday and has experienced her own losses. Both her mom and dad are gone and didn't get to be here this year to welcome her son into the world.

Knowing these sweet ladies are celebrating life on my Scooter's day gives me joy. Joy that even when he is no longer with us they are always a part of our days. There are so many little moments that remind me of Ry from his fun teasing of my mom, which I continue for him to this day, to sharing a recipe that he created just for me. Ryan still has a great big place in my life and in my heart. How lucky I am that I got to be his mom and create so many birthday memories for him. Happy birthday, my son, my Scooter, my Ryan.

In Him,
Joyful

FRIDAY, APRIL 5, 2019

Celebrating with Moments of Grief

Since 1990 I have been lucky enough to share my birthday week with Natalie. Blowing out candles and wishing for a baby girl on April 4th is what God used to bring our sweet daughter into our lives only two days later. On the 5th we went to my grandfather's funeral and my cousin told us about Natalie's birthmom. What a wonderful addition to our family.

Nine years ago we lost our precious son, Ryan, on the 5th of April, right between our birthdays. At first I was convinced that our birthdays would be sad days forever forward. Natalie and I decided to change the narrative and believe that Ry wrapped his trip heavenward in our birthdays. So now we have three celebrations in early April and celebrate Ryan's too short life on the 5th right between celebrating the two of us.

Natalie and Nate gave me a book on Pronoia yesterday. I just completed a writing challenge where I had to write not once, but twice about this word I had never heard before. It is the opposite of paranoia. Believing that everything and everyone is out to bless us. I love that. It seems that is what we did with losing our Ryan. We could wallow in our grief today or reflect on his smile and all the memories we have with him. Of course I hate that my Ry is not here in his daughter's life and with all of us. There is so much he has missed by being

1993

gone too soon. But I love that we have pictures, videos and memories to share on this day that has become Ry's day.

One of the best things about today is sharing my love for my son with others who loved him just as much and still remember. The connections to those people is my warm hug on this day and every day throughout the year. Yesterday Natalie found me not one, but two heart rocks on the shores of Lake Crescent where we are staying. I love that I still get heart rocks even though Ry is not here to find them for me.

Today waves of grief will be a part of my day, but so will connections with others and beautiful memories of a little brown eyed boy and a thoughtful brown eyed man. I love you, my son. I miss you, my Ryan.

In Him,
Joyful

SUNDAY, APRIL 21, 2019

Memories and Easter Moments

We all have Easter memories; Easter traditions that are such a sweet part of our lives. Celebrating the incredible love of Christ with family and friends is so sweet. We do our best to focus on the years we had with our kiddos at home and put aside Easter from nine years ago that was the last one with Ryan. A silent prayer to be thankful for the time we had with him for his twenty-four years gives us a moment to reflect on our loss, but then we think of the gifts he left us with his family. What a blessing our Elissa is, and her daddy sent her an Easter dress that last Sunday of his life that still hangs in my closet.

This year we will sing our hearts out at church and call our families later to hear of all their egg coloring and hunting. The joy in their voices will brighten the day just as the sunrise did this morning. Our hope is in Him, and even though life has its moments that seem too difficult to bear, we never walk alone. We love seeing the Easter pictures and wishes on Facebook. What a gift family and friends are as we celebrate this spring day when Jesus gave all that He had to make it possible for us to be close to Him.
Happy Easter to each of us.

In Him,
Joyful

FRIDAY, NOVEMBER 22, 2019

Then I Opened a Letter

I had a productive positive morning, and then I opened a letter. This morning started with good conversations at occupational therapy for my hand, on to a fourth grade event where I got to be Noni to my Avalon and then off to Santa Fe to take Paula to an appointment and lunch. When I came in the house there on the counter was a letter that we had gotten yesterday but hadn't opened. It was from the Glendale Police Department. Ron and I both assumed it was from Glendale, Arizona since much of our family lives there. He even speculated that they found the truck that our son, Ryan, lost over a decade ago. Yes, he really lost a vehicle. Long story, but true.

So I was half thinking of my Ryan when I opened the letter. It said there was property of ours that was released, and we could claim. My *Mom Eyes* didn't register the date that was right on the page. I began wondering if someone had stolen from Ryan when he lived in Glendale, or if there had been a robbery involving some of my grandfather's guns. Yes, I said guns. To be exact, a handgun and shotgun. After some confusion, clarity came to my protected brain. The date on the letter was April 5, 2010 the day my son shot himself and died. It was not from Arizona but from Glendale, Colorado. The horrid reality was that they were just following up to see if we would like them to release the gun that he used returned to us. Gut punch, tears and desperately trying to reach Ron followed. I was numb with grief that moments ago seemed unimaginable. The guns weren't ours. He didn't live with us. How did they even get our address? Why would they think we would even consider retrieving these weapons? The letter stated that they hoped this reminder would not upset us. That a good deal of time has passed, and we may or may not still be affected by the loss we suffered. What?!? I read and reread those words. Unbelievable. I realize this is a standard letter for getting property back to the rightful owner, but that didn't help as I sat shaking this letter in my hand with tears pouring down my cheeks.

So I have processed with my sister and am sitting here with the letter beside me on the couch. I am okay. Ryan has touched my heart today, not with a lost truck but a horrible reminder of how I lost him. God has me. You all have me. But for now I am just going to sit and listen to his favorite song, watch our videos of him and remember when my Ryan was still able to wrap me in one of his hugs. Today didn't turn out as I'd planned because I opened a letter.

In Him,

Joyful

MONDAY, DECEMBER 16, 2019

Spending the Day with My Mom Through Her Words

Last week I spent an entire day in our 1975 camper van through my mom's eyes. The year was 2000 and all four of our kids were with Ron and I on a two month adventure through Canada and Alaska. I spent the day typing my mom's journal from that once in a lifetime trip. She was faithful to write every day along the way. What a gift she left us to relive our adventure through her thoughts and observations. I was especially

touched as she described her relationship with her grandkids. What a loving lady my mom was to each of us.

She put up with so much on that trip with all seven of us crammed in a 19 foot camper van. Her journal reflected the joy and connections of our time on the road. Never did she complain even when we had to go days between showers and then pay $6 for three minutes of lukewarm water. Natalie, Mom and I would rush to all shower in the same three minutes to save money. What laughter we shared as we got wet, stepped out to soap up and then step under the water to rinse off. We had our routine down to a science by the end. She did comment on what a joy it was to shower in hot water with unlimited time the one day we had to stop at a hotel on the trip home. One of the most annoying aspects of the trip for Mom was that the kids had watched the Austin Powers movie days before we left on our journey. The entire trip was filled with Cam, Ryan and Tanner quoting the obnoxious phrases from the movie. Mom even bet them $5 each that they couldn't go an entire day without mentioning the movie. They did, and Mom had a day of peace at a small cost in her eyes.

Reading my mom's words after losing her last summer was a gift that I cherish. She brought our time together to life and made me smile with her love for my family. My heart is filled with the hope that she and my ornery Ryan are up in heaven reliving times together and having new adventures of their own. I wonder if there is a Mike Myers film in heaven. Mom would say~God forbid.

In Him, *Joyful*

MONDAY, MARCH 2, 2020

My *Birfday* March Second

Happy birthday to Ryan! It feels like I am actually giving my son a birthday gift this year. Sending out books to those who love us about our journey through his death is also a window into his life and love for others. This unedited window to my heart and sharing my son with others is a gift to me and feels like a birthday gift to him. Of course I will send up a balloon as I always have. This year is the first that Ronnie B.

and I won't be together on Ry's birthday. It makes me feel extra lonely that we are not doing this together. But Ron will no doubt get a balloon in New Mexico to lift off as I send mine up in Washington. Maybe we can

FaceTime and send them at the same time. Togetherness is powerful in getting us through missing our son.

This year the other gift is that Natalie's one week old son is named after Ryan. Felix Ryan is doing beautifully and will carry on Ry's name for us. Elissa is a gift to her dad, and so are all the others who continue to love and think about him in their own ways. What a beautiful day it is. I am glad Ryan adored his birthdays. Perhaps he continues to celebrate in his own way in heaven this year. That makes me smile.

In Him,
Joyful

TUESDAY, MARCH 3, 2020

Pity Party to Celebration

So I decided yesterday that attitude is key to getting through a seemingly hard day. Yes, it was Ryan's birthday, and I couldn't call him and sing to him or bake him his favorite cake. But I could celebrate my son in other ways with others who love him as much as I do. My thoughtful niece, Briana, called and told me she would pick up balloons and come by to launch them with me. So after she got off work, Natalie, Nate, Bri, baby Felix Ryan and I went up on the roof in a powerful wind storm believing those balloons would fly sky high. Well, as I videoed the release, Bri let the balloons go, weighted clip still attached. That balloon sunk over the side of this six story building into the alley below. Nate pointed out through our laughter that Ry would have appreciated this nontraditional, unexpected launch. This was the first birthday that Ron and I were not together since Ryan died, so I was having a bit of a pity party earlier in the day, but what a joy to be laughing with family who love my son.

Later in the evening Lissa and I read my blog book posts. I wouldn't be courageous enough to read it on my own. So we are reading it together on FaceTime. We are only getting through a few posts at a time because we take the time to cry and tell additional stories about her daddy. In the background I got to talk to Dorothy and Amalia as well. Oh, how I am blessed to have Ryan's family in my life.

The day started out with me feeling sorry for myself and ended with me

 having the courage to admit the blessings Ryan continues to give me. What a beautiful day it was and what a lucky lady I am to be Mom, Noni and wife to this family God gave me!

In Him,

Joyful

FRIDAY, MARCH 20, 2020

Embracing One More Family Who is Heart-Crushed by Loss

Yesterday we got some news that another family got the heart-crushing news that their son took his life. How it brings me right back to the day we lost our Ryan at his own hand! None of us will ever be able to truly understand the decision to end it all. But it is possible to understand the heartache of those who are left behind. Too many families in our small town can relate to just how devastating the loss of an adult or teen child is from their own personal loss. What I wish is that I could be there for this family to hug them, comfort them and let them know that they are not alone in their grief. Instead, because of the Covid-19 quarantine, I drove past their home and prayed that they could somehow cling to their faith and know that they are loved. This is a family that I am grateful to know having had both their kiddos in my classroom for years.

Families should know that all of us who they share their kids with are so blessed to spend a bit of time with them on their path to adulthood. Especially special ed. teachers who get to walk beside kids for years and elementary teachers who get to make a classroom family of sorts for an entire year. Your loss and pain is real to us as well. We enjoyed your heart for your children at our parent/teacher conferences and while you supported our efforts throughout the year. This loss in our community brings me right back to the loss of my own son. I remember his favorite teacher who put up with him for several years in her special ed. program called me after his goodbye party/funeral and apologized for not being there. She told me that she intended to come. In fact, she was in her car driving up the hill to the church when she was overcome and had to turn around and go home. Her fear was that I would think she was selfish and that she didn't come for us. The reality is I am blessed by her heart for my son who was a little pain in her classroom over a decade before he took his life. The impact of losing a child even when they are grown is hardest on the family. But the loss ripples out into communities and touches so many lives. Those of us who have lived this loss are so sad for one more family joining this group that we would never choose to form. There is no way to really love on a family on a day like today. What I am comforted by is that this family has a great faith, and they will cling to that and each other in the hours, days, weeks and months to come.

For now I will pray and know that even in our Covid-19 isolation we can let them know we love them and grieve with them.
In Him,
Joyful

FRIDAY, MARCH 27, 2020

I Read My Book

I finished reading a book yesterday. That doesn't seem earth shattering since the world is in quarantine, and we have so much time on our hands. Of course it is possible to finish reading a book. But the truth is I finished my book. No, I didn't sit down and write a book. But I did pick up a keyboard and write a blog for the past decade. Leona turned my words into a book for me for Christmas. Then we purchased twenty-four more books to share with those that could pray over this journey of loss. The book she plucked out of my blog was made up of the posts of losing my son to suicide. So you see, reading my own story through loss was difficult to say the least. So yes, I finished a book yesterday. It took me a couple weeks, a few boxes of tissues and a lot of processing and prayer. **As**

of

the printing of this book I lost my beautiful mother in 2019 and my sister, Teri, in November 2020 to Covid. I am once again heartcrushed but know they are up there enjoying Ryan and Dad's antics

But I was so healed by this look back at what God has done through the most life changing event of my life. From the day after Ryan died, I wrote. Not every day and not with an eye for grammar or sentence design. But I wrote out my heart, my faith, my pain and my hope.

Be thankful in all things is a command that Christ gave us in His word. At the beginning of my path through losing my son, I doubted how that would be possible. But looking back on this gift of time and connection was so revealing. Dare I say I am thankful for Ryan's choice a decade ago? Not that he died and left us living life without him. But for the

connections and relationships that are only possible through this loss. Ron and I are here to embrace other families who go through the pain of losing an adult child. This is not a ministry I hoped for, but it is a ministry God has prepared me for. My thought was that statistically when we lost Ryan we would protect other families we love from the same path. The truth is at least a half dozen of our closest friends have endured the same pain we suffered. That we could walk with them through the process of planning a goodbye celebration and be there to just hug them and pray was what I am most thankful for. Trust me, I would have been so content to continue being crazy with middle school kiddos through Young Life. But that is not the ministry God had in mind for me after Ryan died.

Another thing I noticed through reading this book of mine was my faith. Sometimes I have doubted if I ever got off the floor of being a crawling Christian. Looking back I see that I have matured in my faith, and I can trust in that truth. Not that I don't lose focus and try to micromanage on my own, but that I never am on my own in life. That is powerful.

This book is now in the hands of others that I trust to pray for direction as they ignore my grammatical mistakes. God seems to be pressing me to edit and distribute His love for me to a wider audience. I am blessed that Susi and Leona are in this with me. First I thought about paying someone to edit my words, but after careful prayer I believe that I only trust these two with my testimony. So the task has begun to clean up without changing my story. There is a fire in my belly to get this just as it should be. Last night I stayed up until 2:00 a.m. working on it. The time has come to stop thinking some day and make this happen. I believe that if even one person draws closer to Jesus through my heart's words it is worth it. This is not about making money or getting fame but showing the truth. I would rather people know me well than to be well known. That none of us has to walk alone through anything life throws at us. Please pray for direction as I am walking on water with this gift that God has given me. It is His story more than mine. I am just thankful that He pressed me to write before Ryan died so the routine was there to begin the day after I lost him.

God has a plan, and He knew just how much I would need to reflect on His love a decade before I wrote those first agonizing words.
In Him,
Joyful

FRIDAY, APRIL 3, 2020

This Week is Ten Years

The past few days I feel myself steeling for the 5th of the month. I seem to look beyond my birthday to the day of Ryan's departure from this earth and my arms. Sunday will be ten years since the horrific phone call that changed my world. Life has moved past the daily dread of even getting out of bed. This year seems harder than the last few somehow. It may be that being isolated due to this worldwide virus gives me more time to reflect. A friend told me this decade mark is another layer of the onion of grief.

I find myself sort of going over the past ten years; how life has changed and all that has happened in my life. Ryan missed so much. He missed the loss of loved ones and the birth of children. He missed his sweet Lissa growing from a five year old into a beautiful, confident young woman. He missed weddings and family trips. He missed his family, and we missed him. Every gathering has had a hole where his spark should be. This week I have focused on what Ryan has missed, but then my heart will admit that it is really about me missing him. The truth is I want to share life with my son. This sadness is about what I am missing. My son not being in my life this past decade has been central to my life. I don't want to go on without him in my story. I want his goofy smile in my pictures from today, not just those from ten years ago. The past few weeks I have been more pouty about the fact that twenty-four years was not enough time with my son. I thought we would have a lifetime together. Truthfully I feel cheated and want someone to take it back. Rewrite the script. There are other things in my life I can work on and change. I can lose weight, spend more time in prayer, exercise more, reach out to friends and adjust my attitude. Not this. I can't change that Ryan is gone. I can't change that life has gone on without him. The truth is I will never hear his voice at the other end of a phone call. Ten years seems like a week and also a lifetime.

The right things to write about here are the positives that have come out of my son's death. There are certainly relationships and opportunities that are directly because of Ryan. But at this ten year mark the only thing this mama's heart is feeling is loneliness for my son. I am back to obsessively watching videos just to see his laugh and the twinkle in his eye. There are days when it feels impossible to get through the next couple of hours without him. Forget about the next ten years. Time has healed, but even the healing feels like a betrayal. Like life goes on, so did he matter? Did I love him? My head knows the truth that is my mother's heart. This week I am back to being honest about my grief. Back to saying it is okay not to be at my most productive. This week I will get through another milestone in losing my son. This week I will cling to Ron as we both cling to our faith and every precious photo of our boy.

In Him,

Joyful

Cousin Joy!

SUNDAY, APRIL 4, 2020

Birthday Filled with Giving Stops

What a perfect birthday I had yesterday. Ron asked me what I wanted to do for my birthday, and I knew just how I wanted to spend the day and who I wanted to spend it with. So we donned our fabric masks and wiped the grocery store out of Little Debbie cakes and brownies. Ron drove, and I hopped in and out of the Blazer carefully placing these birthday treats on doorsteps all over town. We taped a note to them that said, "I wanted to share my birthday with those I love. Please enjoy this treat from me. Barbara" Ron added a border and balloons to make it even more special. After doorbell ditching I texted to tell them I had left something out front but to feel free to wait a day or two if that made them more comfortable. Coronavirus distancing was strictly in place on our outing.

The best part of my birthday was being able to give to others, and the bonus was spending a day driving around with my Ron. We had a great day with just the two of us doing what was inspired by our Ryan. The last Christmas Ryan was alive he went all over his apartment complex ringing doorbells, wishing people he didn't know Merry Christmas and sharing homemade cookies with them. He and Carolyn spent the day baking any recipes they had the ingredients for and then delivering with pure joy. For my birthday this year Ron helped me be like my son. Of course, I didn't bake these treats. It is a worldwide viral scare, and the right thing to do was to buy prepackaged treats that would be less likely to carry germs. Okay, the truth is I don't enjoy baking as much as Ryan did and buying them made more sense to me.

My joy yesterday came from people responding to our sweet gifts at their door. Yesterday I had so many happy birthday wishes from the almost forty friends who opened their doors after Ron and I drove away and on to the next house on my list. If you didn't receive one I am sorry. We tried to include as many people as we could. All together we spent almost four hours driving around, laughing and enjoying my birthday just being with each other. Yes, this birthday was an extra special one for me. I spent it with my Ronnie B.

In Him,

Joyful

Nana joined Ryan in heaven in January 2015. We miss you every day, Mary.

SUNDAY, APRIL 5, 2020

Ten Years Since Ryan Left Too Soon

Ten years ago today feels like forever and just like it was yesterday. Losing our son, Ryan, has been a path we have walked for the last ten years. This week we reflected on who he was and who we have become from losing him.

I had the opportunity to read my journey when Leona took the part of this blog labeled Ryan and made it into a book for me. I must admit that it took me months to finish reading it. Lissa and I read some to each other over FaceTime. That definitely gave me more courage to

actually read this window into my heart and my grief. Looking back I see a picture of my own faith and peace that Ryan is more than safe in heaven. It also revealed the healing I have had over the past decade. Just how loved I am from all of you who wrapped your physical arms around me has surrounded me with more love than I could have ever imagined. I wrote about the unwanted celebrity that I cringed at after Ryan died. The truth is I didn't want to be that mother who lost her son to suicide. But looking back at this journey shows me how being exactly who I am in this story of my life has brought me love I would never have known without this chapter included. So today I am thankful for the precious years I had with my Ryan, but also thankful for these past ten years of reaching out to others and being held up by them through my story. This is not a story about a mother and her son, but a story of everyone who has loved someone and grieved losing them. Last night I realized that tomorrow Natalie will be thirty years old. Reaching a decade birthday is always a big year. Ten, twenty, thirty and beyond are those milestone years that we celebrate just a bit more than the others. Since Ryan died the day before Natalie's twentieth it will be true throughout my daughter's life that she will share her decade birthdays with the truth of just how long her brother has not been in her life. It is too much for anyone to handle; losing a brother the day before your twentieth birthday. No celebrating, just anguished tears. Now ten years later we celebrate her day, but also wish Ryan could be here to make a most unusual cake recipe for his sister that he loved.

I imagined what I would say at this last post after a decade without Ryan. All I know is that I am okay while not being okay. I feel loved along with feeling lost. There are less waves of grief now than there were ten years ago, but they still come. Thoughts of him are fewer and that makes me sad and angry at times. But the love for him still fills my heart with every heart rock someone gives me or the funky recipes I try. Ryan was my heart. He was also the heart of so many who loved him. Scooter will always be a part of our hearts. It makes me smile as I tell stories of his shenanigans and think of him causing a ruckus in heaven. Heaven wouldn't be heaven if Ryan didn't get to fish, create recipes, prank his grandma and just encourage others with his smile. I don't know exactly what heaven looks like for my son or now for my mom who joined him last summer. But I do know that he makes it a bit brighter even in all its heavenly glory. I am jealous of heaven for getting to have my son instead of me having him here with me. But reading my heart over the past ten years gives me faith that my permanent home will be there with him once again in his mother's arms. Until then I will smile and enjoy the memories that I wouldn't want to live without.

In Him,

Joyful

Ryan Owen Barber March 2nd, 1986-April 5th, 2010. The story is not in his birth or his death but is about all the living and loving in the dash between the two. Our Scooter lives on in each of us.

Special thanks to all who made this book a reality

Lissa and Dorothy~allowing me to share their family story and for always being family. Lissa's precious words about her daddy.

Leona Bjarke~printing my book as a gift and helping me each step of the way.

Susi Shapter~spending hours editing and encouraging.

Nathaniel Madlem~creating the perfect book cover and having patience with me throughout.

Ron - your precious words and always listening to my heart and my words and sharing our life and family for all these decades.

Natalie Barber Madlem~words of love for her brother and family.

Tanner and Cameron Barber~allowing this mom to share their stories and their hearts.

Freedom Elliot - contributing her words and heart to this effort.

Amber Barber~her heartfelt poem.

Justin Nunz ~beautiful song and being our family.

Grace Kiern~sharing her words and heart.

To each of you for your love, support and encouragement along this journey that has been filled with tears as well as laughter and joy.

"What Faith Can Do" Kutless

"By Your Side" Tenth Avenue North

"He's My Son" Mark Schultz

"Could We Start Again Please" Andrew Lloyd Webber

"When Tomorrow Starts Without Me" David Romano

Back Cover

The generous words inscribed on this precious heart rock show how our son impacted the lives of others throughout his own life and even after his death. My hope is that this book will share all of our love for Ryan. I found this heart rock on November 24th, 2020 while I prayed and walked around the Cottonwood hospital. My sister, Teri, was inside struggling for each breath in the Covid ICU. Later that afternoon she took her last breath and stepped into Jesus' arms. Oh, how we all